Biblical Archaeology: A Very Short Introduction

Very Short Introductions available now:

For more information visit our web sites
www.oup.co.uk/general/vsi/
www.oup.com/us

Eric H. Cline

BIBLICAL ARCHAEOLOGY

A Very Short Introduction

OXFORD
UNIVERSITY PRESS

OXFORD
UNIVERSITY PRESS

Oxford University Press, Inc., publishes works that further
Oxford University's objective of excellence
in research, scholarship, and education.

Oxford   New York

Auckland   Cape Town   Dar es Salaam   Hong Kong   Karachi
Kuala Lumpur   Madrid   Melbourne   Mexico City   Nairobi
New Delhi   Shanghai   Taipei   Toronto

With offices in

Argentina   Austria   Brazil   Chile   Czech Republic   France   Greece
Guatemala   Hungary   Italy   Japan   Poland   Portugal   Singapore
South Korea   Switzerland   Thailand   Turkey   Ukraine   Vietnam

Published by Oxford University Press, Inc.
198 Madison Avenue, New York, NY 10016

www.oup.com

Oxford is a registered trademark of Oxford University Press

Cline, Eric H.
Biblical archaeology : a very short introduction / Eric H. Cline.
p.   cm.
Summary: "Archaeologist Cline discusses the origins of biblical archaeology
as a discipline and what first prompted explorers to go in search of sites that
would 'prove' the Bible. He surveys some of the sites, including Hazor,
Megiddo, Gezer, Lachish, Masada, and Jerusalem. Separate chapters deal with
the Hebrew Bible and New Testament, frauds and forgeries, and future
prospects."—Provided by publisher
Includes bibliographical references and index.
ISBN 978-0-19-534263-5 (pbk.)
1. Bible—Antiquities.   I. Title
BS621.C55 2009
220.9′3—dc22
2009006525

9

Printed in Great Britain
by Ashford Colour Press Ltd., Gosport, Hants.
on acid-free paper

To my family and my fellow archaeologists

Acknowledgments

This book owes its existence solely to the efforts and editing of Nancy Toff, to whom I owe a huge debt. I also owe a large debt of gratitude to my students at George Washington University, upon whom I tried out much of this material in my classes over the course of the past eight years, usually without warning them in advance. Grateful thanks are due to Felicity Cobbing, Israel Finkelstein, David Ussishkin, and Shelley Wachsmann for their assistance in procuring or providing some of the illustrations; to Leah Burrows for her bibliographical research assistance; and to Martin J. Cline, Felicity Cobbing, David Farber, Norma Franklin, Jim West, Assaf Yasur-Landau, and several anonymous readers for their helpful critiques, insights, and editorial suggestions regarding earlier sections or entire drafts of this book.

Contents

List of Illustrations

Introduction

The field of biblical archaeology is flourishing today, with popular interest at an all-time high. Millions of viewers watch television documentaries on the Exodus, the Ark of the Covenant, and the so-called Lost Tomb of Jesus. Major publishing houses have published competing Bible atlases, and the popularizing magazine *Biblical Archaeology Review* reaches a large audience. And every year at Easter, Charlton Heston appears on television as Moses in Cecil B. DeMille's classic movie *The Ten Commandments*, raising his arms high to part the waters of the Red Sea so that the Hebrews may cross to safety.

Biblical archaeology is a subset of the larger field of Syro-Palestinian archaeology—which is conducted throughout the region encompassed by modern Israel, Jordan, Lebanon, and Syria. Specifically, it is archaeology that sheds light on the stories, descriptions, and discussions in the Hebrew Bible and the New Testament from the early second millennium BCE, the time of Abraham and the Patriarchs, through the Roman period in the early first millennium CE.

Despite the fact that biblical archaeologists began their excavations in the Holy Land more than a hundred years ago—with a Bible in one hand and a trowel in the other—major questions still remain

1. Israel and Judah from 930 to 720 BCE.

unanswered, including whether there was really an exodus of the Hebrews from Egypt and the extent of David and Solomon's empires. Other unresolved issues involve the specific details of daily life during the period of the Divided Kingdoms, after the time of Solomon, and the difference between Canaanite and Israelite material culture during the Early Iron Age.

Most biblical archaeologists do not deliberately set out to either prove or disprove elements of the Hebrew Bible or the New Testament through archaeology. Instead, they investigate the material culture of the lands and time periods mentioned in the Bible, and the people, places, and events discussed in those ancient texts, in order to bring them to life and to reconstruct the culture and history of the region. This is particularly evident in New Testament archaeology, where the excavation of cities like Caesarea, Capernaum, and Sepphoris has shed light on the social, religious, and geographic situation in the time before, during, and after the life of Jesus.

However, biblical archaeology has generally provided more relevant information that can be correlated with the narratives of the Hebrew Bible than with those of the New Testament. There are several reasons for this disparity. The events depicted in the Hebrew Bible occurred over a much longer time period than those depicted in the New Testament—over millennia rather than over approximately two hundred years. Moreover, the stories and events described in the Hebrew Bible occurred throughout a much larger geographic area than those of the New Testament. The entire Middle East and North Africa provide the backdrop for the stories of the Hebrews, whereas the drama of the early Christians played out mainly in Syro-Palestine and to a lesser extent in ancient Greece and Italy.

For these two reasons of space and time, there are many more potentially relevant Old Testament archaeological sites than New Testament sites. Perhaps of equal importance is the fact that the Hebrew Bible often describes events such as battles and destructions, and solid structures such as buildings and inscriptions carved in stone. These leave behind physical remnants that tend to endure for long periods of time, whereas the narratives of the New Testament more often involved language and ideas that have enormous social impact but leave few physical artifacts that can be discovered by digging. Nonetheless, biblical archaeology has provided wonderful insights into both the Hebrew and Christian Bibles, and correlations with both (see table 1, page 6).

For many scholars, the Bible is an important source of data that helps to shed light on ancient life and practices. Leaving aside for the moment the religious significance and the questions of the historical accuracy of the text, there is no question that the Bible is a historical document of seminal importance. It is an ancient source that often contains abundant details and descriptions of the Holy Land in antiquity. It is a source that can be used—with caution—to shed light on the ancient world, just as Syro-Palestinian archaeologists use Egyptian, Neo-Assyrian, or Neo-Babylonian inscriptions covering the same time period.

This use of ancient sources by biblical archaeologists finds its parallel in the practices of Classical archaeologists who study the texts of the people who lived in ancient Greece and Italy and of New World archaeologists who can now read the texts of the pre-Columbian peoples of the Americas. Classical archaeologists sometimes compare their findings in the field to the Greek and Roman texts, in order to discuss questions such as the nature of the Periclean Building Program or about the plague that ravaged Athens in 430 BCE, while those specializing in the Bronze Age will cautiously use the Homeric texts. In a similar manner, biblical archaeologists often, and with appropriate care, compare their field findings to the biblical account in order to discuss questions concerning David, Solomon, the Divided Kingdoms, and so on.

What is not always known in advance, however, is the accuracy of the accounts either in the Bible or in the Egyptian, Neo-Assyrian, or Neo-Babylonian inscriptions. This problem is not unique to biblical archaeology, for there is considerable variation in the accuracy of the descriptions of ancient Greece and Rome contained in the texts of Homer, Herodotus, Thucydides, the Greek playwrights, the Roman authors, and the Roman historians. As classical scholars readily admit, some texts are more accurate than others. Not all can be used to verify data obtained from field excavations in the Aegean and western Mediterranean.

It is in the question of the historical accuracy of the texts where the interests of professional biblical archaeologists and the educated public overlap, for it is frequently the quintessential biblical questions—the ones that fueled the birth of the field—that still intrigue the public. Did Joshua capture Jericho? Was there someone named Abraham who wandered from Mesopotamia to Canaan? Did David and Solomon exist? Where was Jesus buried? Although biblical archaeology today is a far cry from what it was a hundred or more years ago—it is now more scientifically rigorous, and its practitioners have generally moved on to more anthropologically oriented topics—these basic questions still resonate. Unfortunately, answering them is not always easy.

Table 1. Concordance of Archaeological Data and the Biblical Accounts

Archaeological Finding	Approximate Dating	Biblical Account(s)	Concordance
Excavation of Jericho	1550 BCE	Joshua at Jericho	No
A "destruction layer" at the site of Hazor in modern Israel.	13th century BCE	Israelites burned the city of Hazor during their conquest of Canaan.	Uncertain
The Israel Stele—a textual mention of Israel outside of the Bible.	1207 BCE	Multiple descriptions of the Israelites in the Hebrew Bible.	Yes
Structures at Megiddo, Hazor, and Gezer attributed to Solomon or later kings.	10th or 9th century BCE	1 Kings 9:15: King Solomon levied to build . . . (at) Hazor and Megiddo and Gezer.	Uncertain
Inscription of Pharaoh Sheshonq at Karnak in Egypt and fragment of stele found at Megiddo.	925 BCE	1 Kings 14.25: Attack of Pharaoh Shishak on Judah and Jerusalem.	Probable

The Mesha Inscription, discovered at Dibon in Jordan, naming Omri.	9th century BCE	Multiple mentions of an Israelite king called Omri in the Hebrew Bible.	Yes
Monolith Inscription of Neo-Assyrian king Shalmaneser III, naming Ahab among others.	853 BCE	Multiple mentions of an Israelite king called Ahab in the Hebrew Bible.	Yes
Black Obelisk of Neo-Assyrian king Shalmaneser III, naming and depicting Jehu.	841 BCE	Multiple mentions of an Israelite king called Jehu in the Hebrew Bible.	Yes
Tel Dan Stele in Northern Israel, naming the "House of David."	9th century BCE	Multiple mentions of David, King of United Monarchy in the Hebrew Bible.	Yes
Archaeological finds at Lachish in Israel and the site of Nineveh in Iraq.	8th century BCE	2 Kings 18:13: Neo-Assyrian King Sennacherib attacks the fortified cities of Judah.	Yes

Table 1. (Continued)

Archaeological Finding	Approximate Dating	Biblical Account(s)	Concordance
Siloam Inscription in "Hezekiah's Tunnel" in Jerusalem.	8th century BCE	2 Kings 20:20: preparations made by King Hezekiah of Judah against the coming attack by Sennacherib and the Neo-Assyrians in 701 BCE.	Yes
Tel Migne/Ekron Inscription.	Early 7th century BCE	Ekron, a Philistine city mentioned in the Hebrew Bible.	Yes
Evidence of destruction of Jerusalem, complete with Neo-Babylonian arrowheads.	597 and 586 BCE	2 Kings 24–25; 2 Chronicles 36; Jeremiah 39, 52; and Ezekiel 4: destruction of Jerusalem by Nebuchadnezzar and the Neo-Babylonians.	Yes
Fecal analysis of ancient toilets reveals the diet and parasites of inhabitants subjected to a prolonged siege.	586 BCE	Lamentations 2:20, 4:4, 4:10; Ezekiel 5:10–17: relating to the Neo-Babylonian siege of Judean cities.	Yes
Silver Amulet Scrolls found in the Hinnom Valley in Jerusalem	6th century BCE	Numbers 6:24–26: relating to priestly blessings.	Yes

Item	Date	Description	Verifiable
Dead Sea Scrolls.	3rd century BCE–1st century CE	Contain all books of the Hebrew Bible with the exception of the Book of Esther.	Yes
Temple Mount platform expanded by Herod the Great.	1st century BCE	Matthew 21:12–14: Jesus overturns tables of money-changers in Temple.	Yes
Galilee Boat found on the lakebed of a drought-stricken Sea of Galilee.	1st century BCE–1st century CE	Descriptions of Jesus and followers at Lake Tiberias in the New Testament.	Yes
Inscription mentioning Pontius Pilate, found at Caesarea in modern Israel.	30 CE	Multiple mentions of Pontius Pilate in the New Testament.	Yes
Ossuary of Caiaphas.	1st century CE	John 11:49–53; 18:14: several mentions of Caiaphas, the high priest of the Hebrews at the time of the crucifixion, in the New Testament.	Possible
Megiddo Prison mosaic, with inscription naming Jesus Christ.	3rd century CE	Multiple mentions of Jesus Christ in the New Testament.	Yes

Part I

The evolution of the discipline

Chapter 1

The nineteenth century: the earliest explorers

The first archaeological endeavors in the Holy Land were conducted not by archaeologists but by theologians, biblical scholars, and engineers primarily interested in locating places mentioned in the Bible and mapping the geography of the region. Although none of these men were trained archaeologists, they made important contributions to what would become the field of biblical archaeology.

Pride of place goes to the American minister Edward Robinson. While not the first person to begin working on biblical questions in Palestine (as it was known then), Robinson became the most prominent person of his era to do so. Born in Connecticut in 1794, he was an ordained Congregationalist minister as well as a biblical scholar and explorer. Combining his passions, he toured Palestine in 1838 accompanied by an American missionary named Eli Smith, who was fluent in Arabic. Their goal was to identify as many sites mentioned in the Bible as possible—in other words, to create a historical (and biblical) geography of Palestine. They did so primarily by matching the modern Arabic names to ancient Hebrew names, so that, for instance, they identified modern Beitan as ancient Bethel.

Robinson and Smith succeeded in identifying some one hundred biblical sites during their travels, though they had little more equipment than a compass, telescope, and measuring tapes, plus copies of the Bible in both English and Hebrew. The results of their initial explorations were published in three volumes just a few years later. Robinson returned to Palestine in 1852 and subsequently published another volume. In the course of his work, he not only identified dozens more biblical sites to his own satisfaction but a variety of other remnants from antiquity as well, including an arch at the Temple Mount in Jerusalem, which is still called Robinson's Arch.

Robinson's identifications were not always completely accurate, of course, nor did he succeed in locating all of the ancient sites for which he was searching. At one point, he stood atop Tell el-Mutesellim, a seventy-foot-tall mountain in the Jezreel Valley—which he did not recognize as being man-made—gazing out into the valley towards Mount Tabor and Mount Gilboa, wondering aloud where the famous site of Megiddo (biblical Armageddon) might be. He knew that it must be somewhere close, but it never dawned on him that he was actually standing on it at that very moment and that there were at least twenty different levels of habitation stacked one on top of another within the ancient mound underneath his feet. He was unable to locate either Jericho or Lachish for the same reason, for he never realized that the prominent tells dotting the landscape of the Holy Land were actually the remains of ancient sites.

Soon after Robinson's explorations, the British-based Palestine Exploration Fund (PEF), founded in 1865, hired Charles Warren—a member of the British army who was later knighted and rose to the rank of major general—to explore and record the ancient features of Jerusalem. Beginning in 1867, Warren spent several years engaged in this work, studying the water system and other underground aspects of early Jerusalem. Warren's Shaft—a part of the underground water system of the early city—still bears his name. Long thought to have played a role in David's capture of Jerusalem three thousand years ago, it has recently become clear that Warren's Shaft did not come into use until the eighth century BCE, well after the time of David.

The PEF funded surveys intended to map the geography of all of Palestine, for as the archbishop of York stated at the inaugural meeting of the PEF in 1865: "This country of Palestine belongs to you and to me, it is essentially ours.... We mean to walk through Palestine, in the length and breadth of it, because that land has been given unto us." Moreover, as he said by way of further explanation and justification, "If you would really understand the Bible...you must understand also the country in which the Bible was first written"—a cogent summary of the religious aspect of the motivation for the British.

2. Captain Charles Warren being presented with a book of Samaritan prayers for the archbishop of York by Yakub es Shellaby, head of the Samaritan community. Mount Gerizim, Nablus, 20 April 1867.

There were geopolitical motivations as well. The British were determined to conduct such surveys in the area before the French began to do so. They wished to have a firm grasp of the geography in order to have an advantage when the Ottoman Empire began its inevitable collapse. The British surveys of the 1870s, conducted by the Royal Engineers under the leadership of men such as Captain Charles Wilson, Lieutenant Claude Conder, and Lieutenant Horatio H. Kitchener, resulted in the mapping of virtually all of Palestine. Their work was published as twenty-six volumes of *Memoirs*, a huge map, architectural plans, and photographs.

The work was not easy, however, for the conditions were primitive, and many of the men suffered from malaria; some even died from it. At one point in 1875, while surveying near Safed, the survey team was attacked, and Conder and Kitchener were both badly injured, as were others in their party. The Ottoman authorities eventually captured those responsible and brought them to justice, but the damage had been done. The survey had a lasting impact on the region, which is still felt to the present day, for the modern border between Israel and Lebanon lies at the point where Conder and Kitchener stopped their work in the Upper Galilee.

In contrast to these American and British explorers and engineers, Charles Clermont-Ganneau, a Frenchman who was first sent to Palestine in 1867 to work for the French consulate, was more interested in ancient writings than in architecture or geography. As an epigrapher—a specialist in ancient inscriptions—his primary contribution was the identification of items such as the Mesha Inscription (also known as the Moabite Stone or Mesha Stele), dating to the ninth century BCE and discovered at Dibon in Jordan.

The inscription was commissioned by Mesha, the king of Moab, which at the time was a small kingdom on the eastern side of the Jordan River, in what is now the modern country of Jordan. The inscription, written on a black basalt stone measuring three feet high by two feet wide and describing a victory by the Moabite king, is extremely significant for biblical archaeology, for it mentions "Omri, king of Israel." Omri is known from the biblical account to have ruled over the Northern Kingdom of Israel during the ninth century BCE. The Mesha Stele is one of the first known extrabiblical inscriptions that names a person or place mentioned in the Hebrew Bible.

On the stone, King Mesha lists the major accomplishments of his reign. He probably set up the inscription in connection with the establishment of a temple to the Moabite god Chemosh. Among the items that he mentions are his defeat of the Israelite army, which, according to the slightly different version in the Hebrew Bible (2 Kings 3:4–27), was led by King Jehoram, grandson of Omri of Israel. In particular, Mesha records his recovery of Moabite territory that had previously been seized by Israel. The relevant portion of the inscription reads:

> I am Mesha . . . king of Moab, the Dibonite. My father reigned over Moab thirty years and I reigned after my father. And I built this high place for Chemosh . . . because he saved me from all the kings and caused me to triumph over all my adversaries. Omri, king of Israel, humbled Moab many days . . . but I have triumphed over him and over his house and Israel has perished for ever. Omri had conquered the land of Medeba and he ruled over it during his days and half the days of his son, forty years, but Chemosh returned it in my days.

The modern history of the inscription is fascinating. An Anglican medical missionary by the name of F. A. Klein was the first person to identify the inscription, in 1868. When Klein first saw it in the ruins of ancient Dibon, near the eastern side of the Dead Sea, it was intact. He offered the Bedouin tribesmen the equivalent of $400 for the stone (to which they agreed), but then left it at the site. A year later, an attempt was made by an emissary of Charles Clermont-Ganneau to make a copy of the inscription, but his wet paper tore into several pieces when he left hastily, fearing for his life when a quarrel erupted among the Bedouins.

The Ottoman authorities, who ruled the region, eventually attempted to seize the stone. However, the Bedouin tribesmen—who hated the Turkish governor—tossed the inscription into a large fire until the stone was red-hot and then poured cold water on it. It shattered into hundreds of small fragments, which the Bedouins put into their granaries to avoid handing them over to the authorities.

Eventually, Clermont-Ganneau was able to buy many of the broken pieces. Charles Warren bought a few more, and a German scholar named Konstantin Schlottmann bought yet more. In all, fifty-seven pieces, large and small, were purchased and approximately two-thirds of the original inscription was reconstructed, although it contained many gaps running through individual letters and even whole words. Even with part of the original inscription missing, it remains the longest monumental inscription ever discovered in the Holy Land.

The Mesha Inscription has long been considered important for its confirmation of the existence of the Israelite king Omri. However, the inscription may be even more significant than previously thought, for it may also contain a mention of the House of David (*Beit David*): "…And the house [of Da]vid dwelt in Horonên."

Some years later, Clermont-Ganneau was also involved with another inscription written in early Hebrew. Now called the Siloam Inscription, it was found chiseled into the stone roof of a tunnel in Jerusalem and eventually taken to Istanbul. The tunnel had been dug in antiquity through nearly 1,800 feet of solid rock, from the Gihon Spring outside the city to a location inside called the Siloam Pool. Two boys playing in the tunnel in 1880 looked up at the roof and spied the inscription, which read:

While […] were still […] axe[s], each man toward his fellow, and while there were still three cubits to be cut through, [there was heard] the voice of a man calling to his fellow, for there was an overlap in the rock on the right [and on the left]. And when the tunnel was driven through, the quarrymen hewed [the rock], each man toward his fellow, axe against axe; and the water flowed from the spring toward the reservoir for 1,200 cubits, and the height of the rock above the head[s] of the quarrymen was 100 cubits.

It seemed to Clermont-Ganneau and others that the inscription not only referred to the means by which the tunnel had been constructed but brought to life a passage from the book of 2 Kings in the Hebrew Bible. The passage describes the preparations made by King Hezekiah of Judah against the coming attack by Sennacherib and the Neo-Assyrians in 701 BCE: "The rest of the deeds of Hezekiah, and all his might, and how he made the pool and the conduit and brought water into the city, are they not written in the Book of the Chronicles of the kings of Judah?" (2 Kings 20:20)

The defensive measures implemented by Hezekiah had apparently included digging a new tunnel in order to bring water into the city during a time of siege. A similar strategy had previously been employed at Megiddo, Hazor, and Gezer. Thus the Siloam Inscription not only confirmed a passage in the Hebrew Bible but also helped to explain the probable means by which the earlier water tunnels had been constructed during the Bronze Age at other sites in ancient Palestine.

Making use of all this new information was George Adam Smith, the last but arguably the greatest in the series of historical geographers who contributed to a knowledge of the Holy Land in the years when the discipline of biblical archaeology was in its infancy. Smith, a Scottish theologian born in Calcutta in 1856, is probably best known for his book *The Historical Geography of the Holy Land* (1894), an extremely thorough volume that updated those published by Robinson and other earlier explorers. For instance, Smith was the first to correctly identify Tell el-Mutesellim as Megiddo, after Robinson and others had failed to do so.

Smith wrote his book after two visits to the Holy Land, the first in 1880, when he journeyed through the lands of "Judaea, Samaria, Esdraelon, and Galilee," as he recorded in the preface to the first edition. The second visit was in 1891, when he explored more of the country and even ventured as far north as Damascus. Standing upon the shoulders of those who had gone before him, including Robinson, Conder, and Kitchener, all of whom he cited admiringly, Smith nevertheless ignored a number of their interpretations and contested a number more, as he noted. His aim was to "give a vision of the land as a whole . . . [and] to hear through it the sound of running history."

Smith's volume, which was a resounding success, was republished in a new edition virtually every year through 1931, constantly updated as new archaeological finds were made and new world events transpired. For instance, after General Edmund Allenby captured the site of Megiddo during World War I, Smith added into the 1931 edition an account and translation of the similar capture of Canaanite Megiddo in 1479 BCE by the Egyptian pharaoh Thutmose III. According to one of Allenby's biographers, Sir Archibald Wavell, Allenby had himself carried an earlier edition of Smith's book with him while on his campaigns in Palestine, consulting both it and the Bible on an almost daily basis.

The work conducted by men like Smith, Conder, and Robinson set the stage for what was to come. Once the initial surveys of the geography of the Holy Land had been completed, the next step was to dig into the ground itself, in search of the ancient remains.

Chapter 2
Before the Great War: from theology to stratigraphy

Although Edward Robinson and Charles Warren were pioneers in the field of biblical archaeology, they were not trained archaeologists. Similarly, George Adam Smith was not an archaeologist but rather a theologian, geographer, and historian, while Charles Clermont-Ganneau spent much of his career alternating between diplomatic posts and the exploration of antiquities. For the first "real" biblical archaeologist, one must turn to Sir William Matthew Flinders Petrie. It was primarily through his efforts that biblical archaeology evolved into a rigorous discipline.

Born in England in 1853, just a year after Robinson's second trip to Palestine, Petrie initially honed his archaeological skills in Egypt. He was nearly forty years old when, in 1890, he was hired by the Palestine Exploration Fund and began excavating at the site of Tell el-Hesi, located in what had once been the Southern Kingdom of Judah. There Petrie became the first person in Palestine to excavate according to the methodology of stratigraphy—a seemingly obvious yet profound concept that had its origins in the geological principle of *superposition*.

Unlike Robinson who preceded him, Petrie realized that when succeeding cities are built directly on top of one another, they eventually form a man-made mound, or ancient *tell*—the very tells that could be seen scattered across the landscape of the Holy Land. Moreover, Petrie realized, within those tells, the lower, or deeper, cities will always be earlier in time than the later, or upper, cities. Thus, as Petrie excavated from the top of the mound down, he was proceeding back in time, revealing the history of the tell and the many iterations of the city that lay within it, sometimes uncovering thousands of years and numerous destructions and rebuildings.

Petrie also introduced the concepts of pottery typology and pottery seriation, in which he used the thousands of pieces of broken pottery he uncovered to determine the chronological date of the various levels and of the different cities that lay one on top of another within the mound that he was excavating. Essentially, Petrie realized that pottery types go in and out of style, just as today's fashions do, and can therefore be used to help date the various cities and stratigraphical levels within a single tell.

3. Stratigraphic levels at Tel Kabri in Israel. The history of the Middle Bronze II palace can be seen in the balk, in the form of several plaster floors with occupational layers, lying one on top of another.

He extended this concept to cities and levels in other ancient mounds, both nearby and farther away, reasoning that if similar types of pottery are found at different sites, the levels in which they are found at each site are likely to be contemporary. This point is especially important for eras before the existence of coins, which were not invented until 700 BCE in ancient Lydia, in what is now Turkey.

The results of Petrie's excavations at Tell el-Hesi were published in collaboration with his American partner at the site, Frederick J. Bliss, as a book titled *A Mound of Many Cities* (1894). Petrie's methods and the publication of his discoveries revolutionized the young field of biblical archaeology and firmly established his reputation as one of the founding fathers of the discipline.

Two years later, in February 1896, when excavating in Egypt within Pharaoh Merneptah's mortuary temple, located near the Valley of the Kings across the Nile River from the modern town of Luxor, Petrie discovered an inscription dating to the fifth year of the pharaoh's reign (1207 BCE). Published by Petrie the following year, the inscription—now known as the Israel Stele—is the earliest textual mention of Israel outside of the Bible and is one of the most important discoveries ever made in biblical archaeology. The inscription reads in part:

> The Great Ones are prostrate, saying: "Peace";
> Not one raises his head among the Nine Bows.
> Plundered is Thehenu; Khatti is at peace;
> Canaan is plundered with every evil;
> Ashkelon is conquered;
> Gezer is seized;
> Yano'am is made non-existent;
> Israel is laid waste, his seed is no more;
> Kharu has become a widow because of Egypt;
> All lands together are at peace;
> Any who roamed have been subdued.

The inscription, and its interpretation, has fueled decades of scholarly debates. At the very least, it shows that the Exodus (if it actually occurred) must have taken place by 1207 BCE, since an entity (or people) called "Israel" was present in the land of Canaan by that date.

By the time of Petrie's excavations, additional expeditions to explore the Holy Land were being organized. These explorations were not sponsored by museums such as the Louvre or the British Museum, which undertook excavations in other places in the Near East including the area that is now modern Iraq. Rather, like the PEF, they were sponsored by quasi-national scientific associations such as the Deutscher Verein zur Erforschung Palästinas (DPV)— the German Society for the Exploration of Palestine—which were an extension of imperialistic political movements on the part of the European nations anticipating the demise of the Ottoman Empire's authority in the region. The concept was simple, as the British had previously figured out; if the Ottoman Empire were to collapse, the European countries that already had a presence or interest in Palestine would have the best claim to the territory. "Biblical explorations," including mapping expeditions and preliminary excavations, provided the best excuse—and cover story—for establishing a presence in the area.

One large-scale excavation—quite likely with such imperialistic underpinnings—was undertaken from 1903 to 1905 by the American-born Austrian archaeologist Gottlieb Schumacher, at the site of Megiddo. Known today as the site where biblical Armageddon—the penultimate battle between good and evil—is to take place, as described in the New Testament (Rev. 16:16), Megiddo has been excavated by four different expeditions, of which Schumacher's was the first.

His excavations at Megiddo were conducted on behalf of the DPV and sponsored by Kaiser Wilhelm II, who had visited Jerusalem and the Holy Land in 1898. Unfortunately, Schumacher's methods left much to be desired from a technical point of view, although he did make a number of important discoveries, including the graves of presumed royalty from the second millennium BCE and an inscribed seal belonging to a servant of Jeroboam, one of the kings of the Northern Kingdom of Israel.

Like Heinrich Schliemann, who excavated at Troy in northwestern Turkey just a few decades before (1870–90), Schumacher decided the best way to attack the seventy-foot-tall mound of Megiddo was to employ hundreds of local workmen to dig a huge trench that cut across, and deep into, the entire mound. Portions of the great trench can still be seen today. Just as Schliemann dug right through the level of Priam's Troy for which he had been searching, so Schumacher missed much at Megiddo, including a fragment from an inscription erected at the site by Pharaoh Sheshonq (the biblical Shishak) after his capture of Megiddo ca. 925 BCE. Schumacher's workmen threw the inscribed fragment out on the spoil heap, where it lay among other discarded rocks from dissembled walls until later found and retrieved by the next set of excavators, those from Chicago, in 1925.

Despite the crudity of his excavation methodology, Schumacher was a skilled draftsman with a decent eye for stratigraphy, who created good plans of the remains that he uncovered at Megiddo. Although he published his architectural and stratigraphical discoveries quite promptly, in 1908, it would take another twenty years before the small finds from Schumacher's excavations were published by another German scholar, Carl Watzinger, who is perhaps better known for co-directing his own excavations at the site of Jericho from 1907 to 1909 and again in 1911.

Other excavations were undertaken in this period by the Irish archaeologist Robert Alexander Stewart Macalister on behalf of the PEF. Macalister dug at a number of sites from 1898 to 1909, but his excavation at the site of biblical Gezer, conducted in 1902–05 and 1907–09, was one of the largest in Palestine at the time. Unfortunately, Macalister was the only actual archaeologist working at the site, alongside four hundred workmen and an Egyptian foreman. He dug fast and carelessly, failing to record the precise find spots of most of the objects that he recovered. He apparently did understand stratigraphy, which had been introduced only a decade earlier by Petrie, but was more interested in ancient daily life than in strict chronological ordering. He did not have as much regard for either pottery or stratigraphy as Petrie did, and subsequent work by later archaeologists showed that he had missed much at the site, including misidentifying the age of the Iron Age entrance gate by nearly a thousand years.

Not surprisingly, although he did circulate his results quickly—three large volumes within three years of finishing the excavations—Macalister's publications on his work at Gezer were somewhat lacking. He did, however, successfully excavate a Canaanite "High Place" (a raised altar or hilltop shrine) at the site, which dates back to the Middle Bronze IIB period, ca. 1600 BCE, and consists of ten large standing stones with possible evidence of animal sacrifice. He also found the so-called Gezer Calendar at the site, in 1908. This is an inscription written in paleo-Hebrew (the earliest known version of Hebrew) or possibly Phoenician that probably dates to the tenth century BCE. It describes the principal agricultural activities conducted during the year and thus provides an insight into life during biblical times. It reads: "Two months of ingathering, two months of sowing, two months of late sowing, one month of chopping flax, one month of barley harvest, one month of harvest and completion, two months of grape cutting, one month of summer fruits."

In direct contrast to Macalister, though excavating at approximately the same time, was George Reisner of Harvard University, whom Macalister reportedly detested. Reisner had begun his archaeological career in 1902 excavating in Egypt and the Sudan, especially in the royal cemeteries of Giza, but in 1908–10 he was appointed to lead the excavation of Samaria in Palestine.

4. Reproduction of the Gezer Calendar, found by R. A. S. Macalister at Gezer, Israel, in 1908. Written most likely in paleo-Hebrew and dating to the tenth century BCE, the inscription describes the principal agricultural activities conducted during the year.

Samaria had served as the capital of the Northern Kingdom of Israel during the period of the Divided Monarchy in the first millennium BCE, after the territory ruled by David and Solomon had been split in two following Solomon's death ca. 930 BCE.

Since Reisner had previous commitments for 1908, the director of the team for the first season was Schumacher, who was just a few years removed from excavating at Megiddo. However, Reisner was able to direct the dig for the following two seasons and did a much better job than Schumacher. The team of workmen used at Samaria was almost as large as that used by Macalister at Gezer, usually numbering about two hundred but occasionally rising to as many as four hundred fifty, but the difference lay in the staff. Reisner had assembled a good team, including Clarence Fisher, an architect who would later work at Beth Shean and Megiddo, and they were able to control the workmen and methodically record the finds, both architecture and small objects.

Reisner was well aware of the processes that had created the man-made mounds such as Megiddo and the remains on top of rocky hilltop sites such as Samaria. He saw his mission at the site as an attempt to untangle the human history that lay beneath his feet and ordered early on that one trench be dug as a probe all the way down to bedrock, so that they would have some idea of the complexity of the site and the various strata that they could expect to encounter in other trenches to be dug.

Reisner's documentation of his archaeological excavations and discoveries was more meticulous even than that kept by Petrie and far more than the records kept by Macalister. He was one of the first archaeologists to note that in excavating a site, the archaeologist also destroys it. There is one chance, and one chance only, to excavate any one part of a site. Thus, proper recording was considered essential. Although Reisner was not quick to publish and the results of his excavations at Samaria did not appear until 1924, some fourteen years after the completion of the excavations, they were well done, with good descriptions, beautiful photographs, and understandable architectural plans that can still be used today.

In 1914, just before World War I broke out, the Palestine Exploration Fund hired T. E. Lawrence to conduct an archaeological survey in southern Palestine. Better known today to the general public as "Lawrence of Arabia," from the 1962 biographical film starring Peter O'Toole, Lawrence was an Oxford-trained archaeologist, receiving his degree in 1910. By the time he was hired by the PEF, he had already excavated at Byblos in what is today Lebanon, at Carchemish in what is now northern Syria, and with Petrie in Egypt.

In less than two months, Lawrence and his companion, Leonard Woolley (who would later go on to fame in his own right as the excavator of Ur in Iraq and be knighted for his efforts), managed to survey and record many of the archaeological remains, from all periods, visible in the Negev desert and the Wadi Arabah, all the while ostensibly searching for biblical sites and tracing old caravan routes in an area which the Bible refers to as the "Wilderness of Zin." Unknown to most others, though, was that the archaeological survey was actually a cover for a British military mapping operation, concerned with the overland routes that an invading Ottoman army might take to reach Egypt in the event of war. Military matters aside, Lawrence and Woolley's report of their archaeological findings, titled *The Wilderness of Zin*, was published by the PEF in 1915 and is still used by scholars today; a reprint with a new preface and additional historical material was made available by the PEF in 2003.

By the time World War I ended, biblical archaeology had been transformed from its earliest beginnings, especially through the efforts of men like Petrie and Reisner. However, the discipline was still essentially in its infancy and would soon be transformed once again.

Chapter 3
The interwar period: square holes in round tells

After World War I, Petrie returned to Palestine from Egypt and continued excavating at a number of sites until the 1920s. By this time, he had been eclipsed to a certain degree by new faces and a new chapter in the field of biblical archaeology. This was the period of the British Mandate, during which the British authorities created the first Department of Antiquities in Palestine. At approximately the same time, the British organized the first Department of Antiquities in Jordan and, in the final years of the Mandate, constructed the Palestine Archaeological Museum in East Jerusalem to house all of the finds that had been made to date.

During this period, universities began to replace, or at least to challenge, national organizations in the sponsorship of excavations in the Holy Land. In part this was because many of the new archaeologists working during this period taught at universities, colleges, or seminaries. Frequently their teaching careers and archaeological careers went hand in hand, as they sought proof in the field for their theological beliefs and for their classroom and professional presentations and interpretations of the biblical account. Since these professors taught during the school year, year-round excavations ceased to be the norm and were replaced by excavations conducted primarily during the summers, although there were significant exceptions, such as the site at Megiddo.

This trend has continued to the present day and most foreign archaeologists who work in the area have their home base in either a university or a museum, and excavate during the summers. Many local archaeologists are also professors or curators, although a large number work in governmental establishments such as the Israel Antiquities Authority and the Jordanian Department of Antiquities.

It was in the 1920s that William Foxwell Albright, a professor at Johns Hopkins University, first came to prominence, beginning a decades-long domination of the field of biblical archaeology, including training some of the leading archaeologists, epigraphers, and biblical scholars of the next generation. He is a complex figure—an exemplary excavator, a careful scientist, and a devout Methodist. Albright is frequently referred to as the "dean of biblical archaeology," in part because of the sheer quantity of his writings, the large number of graduate students whom he trained, and his insistence that the Bible was essentially correct, from a historical point of view, and that archaeology could be used to prove it.

Although this is something of an oversimplification of his beliefs, especially since his opinions changed over the decades, Albright was responsible for laying the scholarly groundwork and maintaining the academic integrity of this still-young intellectual discipline. For instance, in large part because of Albright's publications and influence, the first true attempts to divide the history of the Holy Land into proper and discernable archaeological periods were begun. In his publication of Tell el-Hesi several decades earlier, Petrie had referred to the Early, Middle, and Later Jewish Periods. Similarly, when Macalister published the results of his excavations at Gezer in 1912, he classified his finds in terms of a Pre-Semitic and First through Fourth Semitic Periods. In 1922, however, Albright met with three other scholars to devise a proper archaeological chronology— one that took advantage of the so-called Three Age System of classification invented by the Danish scholar C. J. Thompson nearly a century earlier, e.g., the Stone Age, the Bronze Age, and the Iron Age. In the subsequent publication of his excavations conducted at Tell Beit Mirsim (1932), Albright used the new terminology for essentially the first time in a publication concerned with biblical archaeology, further subdividing each of the major periods as necessary. For example, the Bronze Age was divided into the Early, Middle, and Late Bronze Ages, with each of those periods then being subdivided again in turn. Refinement of these periods still continues today (see table 2).

In conducting his research, Albright relied upon a combination of archaeological excavation, textual analysis, and biblical exegesis (a close reading of the text), which is an approach that many still use today. Simply stated, he used the data found during excavations in conjunction with both the biblical text and extrabiblical inscriptions to formulate his conclusions. In so doing, he and his students had to master not only the techniques of archaeology but a number of ancient languages as well, including Hebrew, Akkadian, Ugaritic, and Hittite. His excavations at the site of Tell Beit Mirsim were exemplary, employing Petrie's ideas of stratigraphy and pottery typology/seriation in a fashion not seen before.

Albright used the results of his excavations and other researches to write numerous books, some for an academic audience and some, like *From the Stone Age to Christianity*, for the general public. He frequently split the academic year between Johns Hopkins University, where he was chairman of the Oriental Seminary, and his home at the American School of Oriental Research in Jerusalem (which was renamed the William F. Albright Institute of Archaeological Research in 1970 and is now usually referred to simply as "the Albright"). Albright served as director of the American School for most of the 1920s and 1930s. Established in 1900, the school is the oldest American research center for ancient Near Eastern studies in the Middle East. A number of other foreign-sponsored schools of archaeology were established

Table 2. Archaeological periods in the Holy Land, ca. 8500–586 BCE (adapted from Amihai Mazar, *Archaeology of the Land of the Bible: 10,000–586 BCE* [London: Doubleday, 1992] 30, Table 2).

Archaeological Period	Absolute Date	Major ethnic group or political entity present
Pre-Pottery Neolithic A	ca. 8500–7500 BCE	
Pre-Pottery Neolithic B	7500–6000 BCE	
Pottery Neolithic A	6000–5000 BCE	
Pottery Neolithic B	5000–4300 BCE	
Chalcolithic	4300–3300 BCE	
Early Bronze I	3300–3050 BCE	Canaanites probably present by this time
Early Bronze II–III	3050–2300 BCE	Canaanites
Early Bronze IV/Middle Bronze I	2300–2000 BCE	Canaanites
Middle Bronze IIA (also called MB II)	2000–1800/1750 BCE	Canaanites
Middle Bronze IIB-C (also called MB II and III)	1800/1750–1550 BCE	Canaanites

(continued)

Table 2. (Continued)

Archaeological Period	Absolute Date	Major ethnic group or political entity present
Late Bronze I	1550–1400 BCE	Canaanites
Late Bronze IIA-B	1400–1200 BCE	Canaanites
Iron IA	1200–1150 BCE	Israelites
Iron IB	1150–1000 BCE	Israelites
Iron IIA	1000–925 BCE	United Monarchy of David and Solomon
Iron IIB	925–720 BCE	Divided Kingdoms of Israel and Judah
Iron IIC	720–586 BCE	Kingdom of Judah

(or expanded) in Jerusalem at approximately the same time, including the German Protestant Institute of Archaeology, the École Biblique et Archéologique Française, and the British School of Archaeology.

In the 1930s and 1940s, a new figure on the scene, Nelson Glueck, alternated with and then replaced Albright as the director of the American School. Glueck had arrived in Palestine in 1926, already an ordained rabbi but with a desire to study archaeology. He became Albright's student at the American School and excavated with him at Tell Beit Mirsim, eventually becoming an expert in both pottery and stratigraphy.

Glueck is perhaps best known for conducting a series of surveys and explorations in Transjordan, at that time a relatively unknown area, archaeologically speaking. He advanced the field of biblical archaeology by identifying hundreds of ancient sites in this region, which corresponded to the biblical kingdoms of Edom, Moab, and Ammon. Glueck also surveyed in the Sinai, the Negev, and the Jordan Valley, for in addition to being an archaeologist and a rabbi, he was a spy who worked for the Office of Strategic Services—the predecessor of the CIA. Just as Lawrence and Woolley had surveyed in the Negev as cover for a military operation before World War I, so too Glueck's archaeological surveys before World War II served as cover for determining potable water sources and possible escape routes for the Allied forces to use if the Germans were victorious in Africa and subsequently invaded Palestine.

Particularly during his much later excavations at the site of Gezer, Glueck trained a number of future archaeologists, many of whom are still active in the field. However, he achieved perhaps his greatest prominence when he merged his archaeological training with his rabbinical training, becoming president of Hebrew Union College in Cincinnati, Ohio, a position he held from 1947 until his death in 1971. Although the primary mission of Hebrew Union

College is to train Reform rabbis and cantors, Glueck was convinced that a knowledge of archaeology went hand in hand with a knowledge of the Bible and was instrumental in opening a branch campus in Jerusalem, in addition to a School of Biblical and Archaeological Studies (now renamed the Nelson Glueck School of Biblical Archaeology, located on the HUC campus in Jerusalem).

During this interwar period, James Henry Breasted and archaeologists from the Oriental Institute of the University of Chicago began a major series of excavations at the site of Megiddo. Sponsored by the Rockefeller family, the expedition ran continuously from 1925 until 1939 and stopped only when World War II erupted. This was the longest uninterrupted period of excavation at the site until the current Tel Aviv University excavations began in 1992.

The Chicago excavators lived at the site virtually year round, digging with hundreds of local and Egyptian workmen who sometimes excavated unsupervised while the American archaeologists lay ill with malaria, too sick to get out of bed in the expedition house. When first beginning to excavate at Megiddo, they used a new technique known as horizontal excavation, in which the stratigraphical layers of the tell were "peeled off" one by one, from the top down. Eventually, after painstakingly removing the top two layers of occupation (Strata I and II, dating to the early Hellenistic and Persian periods respectively) and revealing the third layer (Stratum III, dating to the Neo-Assyrian period), the excavators, their money showing signs of running out, had had enough of horizontal excavation and switched to conventional vertical excavation techniques. These included digging a step-trench down the side of the mound, by means of which they eventually reached all the way down to bedrock and were able to ascertain the sequential history of the site. They established that there were at least twenty cities built on top of one another at Megiddo, stretching from 3000 BCE to 300 BCE, complete with palaces, temples, ivory treasures, and plentiful evidence of how the ancient peoples of Canaan and Israel had lived.

During their excavations, the Chicago excavators built a small railroad around the top of the mound, whose sole purpose was to carry away the tons of soil being removed by the workmen. The spoil heaps that were created by the dumping of this soil next to the tell are a prominent part of the Megiddo landscape today—with flowers and grass growing on them in the spring and cows grazing upon them in the summer—and are frequently mistaken by tourists as outlying sections of the ancient site, which they are not. It was on one of these mounds that a local kibbutznik, grazing his sheep and goats during the 1950s, found a fragment of the Epic of Gilgamesh inscribed on a clay tablet. Clearly, like Schumacher before them, the Chicago excavators occasionally missed ancient artifacts, which then wound up on, or in, the spoil heaps of removed earth.

The Chicago archaeologists thought they saw the handiwork of Solomon at Megiddo. They identified several buildings at the site as stables, citing in particular the description in 1 Kings of "chariot cities" belonging to Solomon: "And Solomon gathered together chariots and horsemen; he had fourteen hundred chariots and twelve thousand horsemen, whom he stationed in the chariot cities and with the king in Jerusalem" (1 Kings 10:26). The proper identification of these buildings was the source of debate among archaeologists for the remaining decades of the twentieth century. While some agreed that these were stables, others saw them as storehouses, barracks, marketplaces, or fulfilling some other unidentified purpose. In 1998, the Tel Aviv University expedition to Megiddo uncovered another "stable" at the site and settled the debate by identifying numerous features that circumstantially point to stables as being the correct identification. Unfortunately it is by no means clear that these stables were built by Solomon. They could have been built by Omri, Ahab, Jeroboam II, or any one of a number of other kings who lived and ruled in the Northern Kingdom of Israel long after Solomon died.

Interestingly, at the same time that the Chicago archaeologists were excavating at Megiddo, a consortium of other archaeologists known as the Joint Expedition was excavating not too far away, having renewed excavations at the site of ancient Samaria, which had once been the capital of the Northern Kingdom of Israel and which had earlier been the focus of Reisner's Harvard University expedition. As part of this new expedition, archaeologists from the British School of Archaeology in Jerusalem, the Palestine Exploration Fund, and the Hebrew University of Jerusalem, as well as several other institutions, dug at the site from 1931 to 1935. Among these archaeologists was Kathleen Kenyon, who had begun her archaeological career working in South Africa with Gertrude Caton-Thompson and in Britain with Mortimer Wheeler. This was her first excavation in Palestine, though she would later go on to greater fame by excavating at Jericho and Jerusalem.

When Kenyon joined the team to help excavate Samaria, she brought with her a revolutionary method of excavating, which had been developed in Britain by Wheeler. In this system, excavators pay careful attention to differences in the color, texture, and other characteristics of the soil and of the ancient remains. The collection buckets (or boxes) for pottery and artifacts are changed every time a difference is noted, thereby allowing the digging to be done according to the observable stratigraphy (as opposed to digging rigidly, ten centimeters at a time, as some earlier excavators had done). Moreover, the excavating is done in squares measuring exactly five meters by five meters, with one-meter-wide sections—known as balks—left standing between the squares. These balks not only serve as paths for the archaeologists and workers to walk upon, but their vertical faces—called "sections" (as in cross-sections)—clearly show the history of the excavated area. Layers upon layers are drawn and photographed at the end of the season and subsequently published in the excavation reports,

5. Overhead of Areas K and Q at Megiddo, end of the 2008 season. The use of Kenyon-Wheeler 5m x 5m squares in a grid pattern, with one-meter-wide balks between, can be clearly seen.

allowing the stratigraphy of the site to be examined and reexamined as necessary, not only by the original excavators but by subsequent archaeologists as well.

This new, more precise method of stratigraphical excavation, which is arguably the most accurate and sensitive means of digging, became known as the Kenyon-Wheeler method of excavation. It is still the principal method used by archaeologists digging in the Holy Land and elsewhere, although it has been modified to a certain extent by some Israeli archaeologists who use it in conjunction with broad horizontal excavations, to expose more of a single layer of the site at one time in a controlled manner.

Chapter 4
After 1948: biblical veracity and nationalism

Biblical archaeology entered a new phase after the end of World War II, and more precisely after the Israeli War of Independence of 1948. It was a phase known for the re-examination and excavation of sites that contained possible links between ancient Israelites and modern Israelis, in order to both construct a national narrative and continue to explore the veracity of the biblical account.

In 1951 Kathleen Kenyon was appointed director of the British School of Archaeology in Jerusalem (now renamed the Kenyon Institute in her honor) and soon thereafter began work at the site of Jericho. Her excavations there from 1952 to 1958 employed the successful Kenyon-Wheeler method of vertical excavation, resulting in some very important discoveries.

Kenyon had been asked to excavate at Jericho because of questions that had been raised by John Garstang's previous excavations at the site from 1931 to 1936. Garstang had not been the first to dig at Jericho, for Charles Warren, Ernst Sellin, and Carl Watzinger had all excavated there before him, but contrary to those previous excavators who dated the destruction of City IV at the site to 1550 BCE, Garstang suggested that the city had been destroyed in about 1400 BCE, specifically by Joshua and the invading Israelites, as described in the biblical account (Josh. 6:1–20). However, his announcement of this interpretation met with severe criticism from some quarters—in fact, it has been described as the most famous faux pas in the history of biblical archaeology—so he asked Kenyon to recommence the excavations in order to check his results and conclusions.

Garstang based his date for the destruction of Jericho in part upon an absence of imported Mycenaean pottery from Greece at the site. Such pottery is commonly found at Canaanite sites in the fourteenth and thirteenth centuries BCE; that there was none at Jericho meant, according to Garstang, that the city must have been destroyed before this period, i.e., by the year 1400 BCE. Garstang believed that the city wall had fallen as the result of an earthquake at that time and that the city had been destroyed by the invading Israelites, who had presumably taken advantage of the earthquake.

Using her superior excavation methods, Kenyon established that the site had indeed been destroyed about 1550 BCE, as the previous excavators thought, rather than 1400 BCE, as Garstang suggested. In addition to the lack of imported Mycenaean pottery from the fourteenth and thirteenth centuries BCE, she pointed out that there was also a lack of pottery from the earlier LB I (Late Bronze I) period, dating to 1550 to 1400 BCE, which suggested that the site had been destroyed at the beginning of that period rather than at the end. As for the city wall that Garstang had found, it may have been destroyed by an earthquake, but it did not belong to City IV. In fact, its destruction had taken place a thousand years earlier, about 2400 BCE.

According to Kenyon's findings, Jericho had remained essentially deserted for the rest of the Late Bronze Age and into the early part of the Iron Age. It was therefore uninhabited at the time of Joshua and the coming of the Israelites. Thus, the archaeological findings and the biblical account are asymmetrical (or inconsistent with each other) at a site fundamentally important to the account of the Israelite conquest as Jericho. Although the debate over Jericho continues to this day, only a few biblical archaeologists still agree with Garstang's position; the rest agree with Kenyon.

In fact, Garstang himself came to bitterly regret linking his excavation data from Jericho to the biblical passages concerning Joshua's capture of the city. He was a careful archaeologist who served as the first director of the British School of Archaeology in Jerusalem and instituted British policy toward antiquities in the region. He was also one of the scholars who worked with Albright in 1922 to create the chronological terminology used henceforth in the field. It is quite possible that Garstang was unduly influenced by his own wife, who wrote the chapter linking Jericho's destruction to Joshua, and by the primary sponsor of his excavations, Sir Charles Marston, who sought to use archaeology to prove the Bible. If so, this may be the earliest example of a sponsor possibly affecting or influencing the interpretation of excavation data, which is still considered to be a potential problem in current biblical archaeology.

Besides Samaria and Jericho, Kenyon excavated in Jerusalem for a number of years, beginning in 1961. Her most important discovery in the area was that of the so-called Stepped Stone Structure, which is usually thought to have been part of the original Jebusite (or Canaanite) defensive system of the city, dating back to the Bronze Age. Unfortunately, she died before fully publishing the results of her excavations at Jericho and Jerusalem, and it would be decades before other scholars published the results for her.

Apart from Kenyon, perhaps the best-known biblical archaeologist active during this immediate postwar period was Yigael Yadin. Yadin had three full careers: As a military leader, he served, among many other duties, as chief of staff of the Israel Defense Forces (IDF). As a politician, he served as deputy prime minister in the government of Menachem Begin. As an archaeologist, he was a faculty member of the Hebrew University of Jerusalem.

His military and political careers notwithstanding, Yadin was quite literally born to be an archaeologist. He was the son of Eliezer Sukenik, the Hebrew University of Jerusalem scholar who bought the first three Dead Sea Scrolls in 1947, when Yadin was a thirty-year-old university student. After serving as Head of Operations during the 1948 war and then as chief of staff of the IDF, Yadin went back to school, eventually writing his PhD thesis on the translation of the Dead Sea Scrolls.

Later, as a university professor and mentor, Yadin taught an entire generation of future archaeologists and initiated or restarted excavations at many sites, including Megiddo. He was not only interested in establishing an Israeli national identity with regard to ancient evidence for a Jewish presence in the land, but—like his American counterpart Albright—thought that archaeology could help prove the accuracy and authenticity of the Bible.

Yadin's first substantial excavations took place at Hazor, located in the north of Israel. The British archaeologist John Garstang had already dug there in 1928, but it was Yadin whose excavations from 1955 to 1958—undertaken on behalf of the Hebrew University of Jerusalem and sponsored in part by the Rothschild family— brought the site to life. Yadin enjoyed the unflagging support of David Ben-Gurion—the first prime minister of Israel—because his excavations helped Ben-Gurion to create an identity for the new state of Israel. The Hazor excavations were essentially a national effort, with the workmen supplied by the state. Yadin's staff members were among the best available; many of his area supervisors, in charge of separate portions of the dig, went on to become established professors of archaeology or key figures in the Department of Antiquities.

At the site, Yadin uncovered the remains of a huge Canaanite city that had flourished during the Middle and Late Bronze Ages, and especially during the second millennium BCE. He concluded that Hazor was a major metropolis, a city that was mentioned in texts written as far away as Mari in Mesopotamia during the eighteenth century BCE. The city, during this early period, was protected by a massive sloping earthen rampart, known as a *glacis*, which was ninety meters wide and fifteen meters high. The glacis gave the site a distinctive shape, which can best be seen today when approaching from the south.

At Hazor, Yadin also uncovered the remains of a city dating to the Late Bronze Age and probably specifically to the thirteenth century BCE, which had been destroyed by fire. Based upon his dating of this destruction, from pottery and other artifacts found in the ruins, Yadin attributed the burning of this city to the invading Israelites who, according to the biblical tradition, captured and burnt Hazor during their conquest of Canaan (Josh. 11:10–13). This confirmed, for him, the biblical accounts of the Israelite conquest of Canaan and, therefore, the claims of modern Jews to the ancient land of Israel.

Yadin also excavated at Megiddo. Following on the heels of Gottlieb Schumacher (1903–1905) and the University of Chicago (1925–1939), Yadin headed the third expedition to the site, which took place during a few brief seasons in the mid-1960s and early 1970s. He used the Megiddo excavation to train his graduate students, just as he had done earlier at Hazor. Moreover, he used the excavations as an opportunity to investigate his theories about the authenticity of the biblical tradition.

At Megiddo, Yadin uncovered the ruins of buildings and other constructions, including a city gate and a palace. He identified the palace on the basis of its architectural plan as a "bit hilani"—a Mesopotamian name for a specific type of palace more usually found in northern Syria at the time of Solomon. The nearby city gate, with six chambers, was attached to a casemate wall (consisting of parallel inner and outer defensive walls connected by internal constructions to create small rooms that function both as part of the wall and as storage or living spaces).

6. Yigael Yadin at Megiddo in January 1960. Sitting (*at the top*): David Ussishkin (student at that time; now co-director of the excavations); standing, from *left*: Yigael Yadin, Avi Eitan (later director of antiquities), Avivah Rosen (secretary of the archaeology department of the Hebrew University), Immanuel Dunayevsky (architect), and Ariel Bermann (student at that time).

Earlier, at Hazor, Yadin had located part of a casemate wall and a city gate very similar to those which he now found at Megiddo. He dated all of these structures to the time of Solomon in the tenth century BCE, in part because of one passage from the Bible—a passage from 1 Kings that describes the building activities of Solomon at the sites of Megiddo, Hazor, Gezer, and Jerusalem: "And this is the account of the forced labor which King Solomon levied to build the house of the LORD and his own house and the Millo and the wall of Jerusalem and Hazor and Megiddo and Gezer" (1 Kings 9:15).

Yadin decided to see if there was a similar city gate at Gezer, the final site mentioned in the biblical passage. Gezer had been excavated previously, from 1902 to 1905 and 1907 to 1909, by the

Irish archaeologist Robert Alexander Stewart Macalister. Yadin therefore began excavating through Macalister's records rather than through the actual dirt. And, he found what he was looking for—a city gate strikingly similar to those at Megiddo and Hazor. Macalister had found one half of it but had identified it as a Maccabean fortress or palace, dating it to the second century BCE and the revolt led by Judah "the Hammer" Maccabee. Yadin believed that Macalister had misidentified this structure and that rather than being a Maccabean fortress or palace, it was instead half of a city gate, complete with side chambers just like those at Megiddo and Hazor. However, the other half still remained to be uncovered.

At the time of Yadin's researches, the Hebrew Union College-Jewish Institute of Religion in Jerusalem together with the Harvard Semitic Museum had already reopened the excavations at Gezer. Yadin contacted the American archaeological team excavating there and explained his theory to them. Sinking their picks and trowels into the dirt, they quickly found the other half of the gate, thereby confirming his hypothesis.

These initial American excavations at Gezer lasted for ten years. It was there that the system of having American college students serve as volunteers on the excavation in return for receiving college credit was first officially instituted on a large scale. This practice, which helps to bring in needed dollars to run the excavations, is now commonplace at every major excavation in Israel, as well as at many in Jordan, Syria, Turkey, Greece, and Egypt. By the 1960s, additional money for excavations like Gezer began to stream in from private donors, philanthropic organizations, and eventually, grants from scientific and government foundations such as the National Science Foundation and the National Endowment for the Humanities. All these continue to serve as prime funding sources, including at Gezer, which is now once again being excavated, this time by a joint American-Israeli team.

Yadin's excavations at Hazor and Megiddo were successful in uncovering new material, but it was his excavations at Masada, the desert fortress besieged by the Romans in the aftermath of the First Jewish Revolt (66–70 CE), that brought him worldwide attention. The excavations lasted only from 1963 to 1965, but they involved an international team of archaeologists and used volunteers on a scale that had not previously been seen at any excavation in Israel. Although it is not technically a biblical site, except insofar as it was fortified by Herod the Great in 40 BCE, Masada looms large in the archaeology of the region, for it has been a symbol of Israeli nationalistic identity and debate since its excavation.

Masada rises some 1,300 feet above the surrounding arid landscape, near the southern end of the Dead Sea, thirty miles southeast of Jerusalem. The mountain fortress on its top gave shelter to Herod's mother and fiancée while he was in Rome in 40 BCE seeking support for his rule over Palestine from Mark Antony and the Senate. Herod saw the site as a possible place of refuge for himself and his family, and he outfitted it with two palaces, a number of water cisterns, barracks for soldiers, and storehouses for supplies. He never actually used it as a fortress, and the site achieved its greatest renown just over a century later, in 70 CE, when Jewish rebels known as the Sicarii (Dagger-Men) took it over after the failure of the First Jewish Revolt and the destruction of Jerusalem by Roman armies commanded by Titus.

From 70 to 73 CE, the Jewish rebels occupied Masada, conducting raids for food in the surrounding countryside. Finally the Romans decided to rid themselves of the pesky Jews once and for all. The resulting action is told in great detail by Flavius Josephus, the Jewish general turned Roman historian. According to Josephus, the Romans besieged the site, building several camps and a wall on the desert floor, completely encircling the mountain fortress, in order to prevent the occupants from obtaining food and supplies. The Romans then built a massive ramp up the side of the mountain and wheeled their war machines directly to the summit. They soon breached a hole in the defenses and prepared to enter the site. However, night was falling and the Romans postponed their attack until the next morning. During the long hours of that night, which took place during Passover of the year 73 CE, the Jewish defenders of Masada decided to take their own lives rather than be captured by the Roman troops. Some 960 Jewish defenders died by their own hand. When the Romans entered the next morning, they found only a few survivors who had hidden in an empty cistern and emerged to tell the tragic tale.

There are, though, some questions about the accuracy of Josephus's narrative. Several mistakes made by Josephus in his recounting of the events have long been noted by historians of ancient Israel— for instance, he mentions only one palace on top of the site, as opposed to two, and gives the wrong heights for the walls protecting the summit of the mountain—and it is generally accepted that he was not physically present during the siege and capture of Masada. Most likely, Josephus wrote his account safely back in Rome, utilizing the day books and other primary sources provided by Flavius Silva, the Roman commander who captured the site.

Yadin decided to excavate Masada in large part to establish what really happened there nearly two thousand years ago. The physical difficulties created by the 1,300-foot-tall mountain made the excavation unique. Heavy equipment had to be lifted to the top of the mountain by helicopter; volunteers had to walk up the long and winding Snake Path every morning and come back down it every evening. But Yadin, and soon the world, declared the effort to be worth the investment. The team uncovered numerous structures, including two palaces, a tannery, storerooms, and cisterns, as well as artifacts of everyday life such as a man's belt buckle, which allowed them to glimpse what life had been like for the occupants in the days and weeks before they died.

Perhaps most importantly for Yadin, the excavators found remnants of a conflict—piles of sling stones, arrowheads, and other weapons. They discovered several bodies, including one group of three bodies that Yadin interpreted as the remains of a husband, wife, and child. Other bodies were found in a cave on the side of the cliff. The findings of the excavation transfixed the citizens of Israel and were noted far beyond the borders of the new state. Yadin created a national narrative, based on the belief that his excavations corroborated Josephus's account. For several decades thereafter, new recruits were sworn in to the Israeli army in a ceremony conducted on top of Masada, declaring that "never again" would Masada fall.

But in recent years, Yadin's interpretation of his excavation has been called into question, most prominently by Nachman Ben-Yehuda, a professor of sociology and anthropology at Hebrew University in Jerusalem. In two books and a number of articles, Ben-Yehuda and other experts, including physical anthropologist Joe Zias, have explored some of the problems in Yadin's interpretation and have revealed possible inaccuracies and misinterpretations. Principal among these are the discovery that the "family group" uncovered by Yadin may not have been a family group at all but simply several unrelated individuals, and that the bodies found in the cave may be those of Roman soldiers rather than Jewish defenders. The debate and the controversy about Masada and the question of whether the suicide by the Jewish defenders ever took place still continue. The Israeli army has ceased to swear in its new recruits on top of Masada.

Chapter 5
Beyond the Six-Day War: new surveys and strategies

The period after the Six-Day War in 1967 saw a new phase in biblical archaeology, generated in large part by Israel's capture of lands previously belonging to Jordan, Syria, and Egypt. A new generation of Israeli archaeologists began wide-ranging surveys, and a few excavations, in territories encompassing the biblical regions of Judaea and Samaria, which before the Six-Day War were beyond the borders of Israel and thus off limits to Israelis. A number of additional projects were begun by international archaeologists in Jordan at this same time, including at biblical sites such as Heshbon and Dibon, but the results were not nearly as revolutionary as those in Israel.

The new emphasis on surveys was part of a larger worldwide archaeological movement in the late 1960s and early 1970s. This movement, known as the "New Archaeology" or "Processualism," was spearheaded by the American Lewis Binford and his students. It attempted to emphasize archaeology as more of a "hard" science, with a particular effort toward generating universal laws about the past. Surveys were seen as one of the ways to do this inexpensively and effectively.

In this type of archaeological survey, a team usually consisting of between five and fifteen members—far fewer than the numbers needed on an excavation—walk across the land with their eyes fixed on the ground, recording what they see. The recorded items may include pottery fragments, stone scatters, ancient walls and foundations, and other materials of potentially ancient origin. This technique may be applied to document every site in a given region, regardless of its time period. The results provide an insight into the complete history of the area being surveyed, with the numbers of sites from each period reflecting the fluctuations in population density.

The Holy Land, and especially Israel, was of course no stranger to archaeological surveys. In addition to the earlier, and more primitive, surveys conducted by Glueck, Lawrence, Kitchener, Conder, and Robinson, Yohanan Aharoni—Yadin's archnemesis and the eventual founder of the rival Institute of Archaeology at Tel Aviv University—had initiated a well-known survey in the Galilee during the 1950s. Now, a new round of surveys was begun after the Six-Day War, especially in the West Bank and the Sinai, conducted by the Israel Department of Antiquities. The best-known of these major surveys were the "Emergency Survey of Judaea, Samaria, and the Golan," directed by Moshe Kochavi on behalf of the Israel Exploration Society, which began in 1968, and the "Emergency Survey of the Negev," directed by Rudolph Cohen from 1978 to 1988. Eventually, working from the late 1960s through the 1980s, Israeli archaeologists such as Adam Zertal, Avi Ofer, and Israel Finkelstein found literally hundreds of sites from biblical periods, none of which had been previously identified. As a result, estimates of population based upon site number and size for periods such as the Iron Age—during the Divided Kingdom phase (ca. 930–586 BCE)—were changed and updated for both the Northern Kingdom of Israel and the Southern Kingdom of Judah.

It became clear, for instance, to judge from the large number of new sites discovered during the surveys, that there were far more people living in the Northern Kingdom of Israel at the time of the

Neo-Assyrian invasions from 734 to 720 BCE than had been thought previously. It was also clear that the population of the Southern Kingdom of Judah increased dramatically in the final decades of the eighth century BCE, probably as a result of refugees pouring in from the Northern Kingdom as the Neo-Assyrians invaded. These findings were significant for biblical archaeologists intent on learning what life had been like in these areas during the first millennium BCE.

The Six-Day War resulted not only in the capture of vast lands in the West Bank and the Sinai, but in the capture and occupation of the Old City of Jerusalem by Israeli forces during the war. The subsequent demolition and construction projects in the city enabled Israeli archaeologists to make important discoveries as they excavated in areas that had previously been inaccessible to them. In particular, the new excavations indicated that there had been substantial new development and construction in the city of Jerusalem in the last few decades of the eighth century BCE. The population of the city seems to have jumped from one thousand to about fifteen thousand inhabitants during this period, and the entire region went from a sleepy backwater to an important part of the ancient Near East in a very short span of time, again probably as a result of refugees arriving from the Northern Kingdom between 734 and 720 BCE.

Working in the Jewish Quarter of Jerusalem as well as by the Temple Mount and in the City of David, archaeologists such as Nahman Avigad and Benjamin Mazar uncovered evidence of tremendous destruction in the city during the early sixth century BCE. They found ash and debris piled high, and blocks of stone that once supported buildings lying about torn and broken. In the debris, they found arrowheads of a type specifically used by the Neo-Babylonians in the sixth century BCE. These findings confirmed the brief accounts given in the Hebrew Bible (2 Kings 24–25; 2 Chron. 36; Jer. 39, 52; Ezek. 4), and the longer and more dramatic account written centuries after the event by Flavius

Josephus (Josephus, *Antiquities of the Jews* 10.7.108–10.8.154), concerning the destruction of Jerusalem by Nebuchadnezzar and the Neo-Babylonians in 586 BCE.

Intriguingly, the archaeologists found several ancient toilets whose contents they were able to examine under a microscope. The microscopic analysis revealed that the inhabitants had been eating so-called "backyard plants"—mustard, radishes, cabbage, parsley, coriander, and the like. Some had suffered from tapeworm and whipworm, intestinal parasites that are acquired as a result of unsanitary and unhygienic conditions and practices—such as using human manure as fertilizer, not having enough water for thorough rinsing, and not having enough fuel to cook meat thoroughly. Archaeologists studying the data suggested that the inhabitants were under some sort of environmental stress. The eighteen-month-long siege and subsequent destruction of the city by the Neo-Babylonians in 586 BCE, as reflected in the Hebrew Bible (Lam. 2:20, 4:4, 4:10; Ezek. 5:10–17), seems the obvious culprit.

The Jewish Quarter of Jerusalem also yielded evidence of a destruction that took place nearly seven hundred years after the Neo-Babylonian invasion, during the Roman conquest of Jerusalem. Here Avigad uncovered the "Burnt House," so-called because it was the remains of a house that had burned down during the First Jewish Revolt (66–70 CE), which contained the remains of a young woman—an arm and a hand only—along with a spear and various objects that identified the owners of the house.

Elsewhere in Israel, a new set of excavations was initiated in 1971 at Tell el-Hesi, the site that had been first excavated by Petrie nearly a century earlier. The new expedition was led by Larry Toombs, a professor at Wilfred Laurier University in Canada. Toombs had dug with Kenyon at Jericho in the 1950s and brought the Kenyon-Wheeler method of excavation with him, first when he dug at biblical Shechem with G. Ernest Wright of Harvard University in the 1960s and then when he reinitiated the excavations at Hesi in the 1970s. He thus served as an integral link in the chain from Wheeler and Kenyon to present-day excavators in the Holy Land. However, he introduced a few new and notable concepts that are still used to this day on many American, Israeli, and Jordanian expeditions.

First among these is the idea of drawing a daily topographic plan of each area being excavated at the site, so that the daily progress can be followed and a record compiled as objects and architectural elements are discovered and then removed; the scale used ranges from 1:20 to 1:100, depending upon the size of the area being excavated. Second is the idea of individual loci, in which each distinctive feature discovered during the excavations is given a separate locus number, while basket numbers are used to further define either minute changes within loci or differentiation in elevation. These are all then recorded on individual locus sheets, which include a description of the locus, relevant measurements and elevations, and a graphic description of each of the baskets that make up the locus. The paperwork thus generated serves not only as a record during the excavation but as detailed documentation, which facilitates the final publications of the expedition and allows other archaeologists to later reconstruct, and sometimes to reinterpret, the findings that have been made. The original paper locus sheets invented by Toombs have now been replaced by computer databases and online entry, but the general idea still remains the same. Finally, Toombs believed that it is imperative to publish all of the data that an excavation team uncovers, so that others can use it as well.

Despite all the success enjoyed by biblical archaeology following the Six-Day War, one of its leading practitioners, William G. Dever of the University of Arizona, began to question the validity of this field of study. As early as 1972, Dever attempted to rid the profession of the name "biblical archaeology" and to introduce in its place what he considered to be a more accurate name,

"Syro-Palestinian archaeology." Arguing that archaeologists were no longer primarily interested in proving or disproving the Bible, but were now using their methods to shed light on the various peoples and cultures of the ancient Near East, Dever went on a decades-long crusade to delete the words "biblical archaeology" from the lexicon. Due in part to this effort, the name of the semipopular journal published by the American Schools of Oriental Research—the premier professional organization for Near Eastern archaeologists in the United States—was changed from *Biblical Archaeologist* to *Near Eastern Archaeology* in 1997. However, not all agreed with Dever. Amnon Ben-Tor, of the Hebrew University of Jerusalem, wrote in the introduction to his classic edited volume on ancient Israel: "Eliminate the Bible from the archaeology of the Land of Israel in the second and first millennia BCE, and you have deprived it of its soul."

Important new excavations began during the 1980s, especially by the second generation of Israeli archaeologists—including David Ussishkin, Israel Finkelstein, Amihai Mazar, Roni Reich, Adam Zertal, and others—at biblical sites such as Shiloh, Izbet Sartah, and Giloh. In the excavations conducted from 1981 to 1996 at the site of Tel Miqne, directed by Trude Dothan of the Hebrew University of Jerusalem and Sy Gitin of the Albright Institute in Jerusalem, cadres of American, Israeli, and international volunteers were used, on occasion digging at night under floodlights to avoid the heat of the day. Advances in the discipline, stemming from the influence of the New Archaeology, meant that the excavators were supplemented by specialists in paleoethnobotany, physical anthropology, palynology, archaeozoology, and other disciplines in which the study of minutiae recovered from the excavation sheds additional light on daily life in antiquity.

Similarly, Larry Stager's excavations at the Philistine site of Ashkelon, conducted on behalf of Harvard University and the Leon Levy Foundation and stretching over the course of more

7. Israel Finkelstein at the Megiddo excavations in northern Israel, where he has been co-director since 1992. Finkelstein is the Jacob M. Alkow Professor of the Archaeology of Israel and former director of the Sonia and Marco Nadler Institute of Archaeology at Tel Aviv University.

than twenty years (since 1985), produced much new data concerning Ashkelon's archaeological record. He was able to trace the history of the site from its days as a Bronze Age port through its several destructions at the hands of invaders, including the Neo-Babylonians in the late seventh century BCE, and then into the Persian period and beyond.

Perhaps the best-known artifact coming from Stager's excavations is a statuette of a silver calf, dating to the Middle Bronze Age. The statuette was discovered during the final days of the 1990 season at Ashkelon, within a pottery vessel shaped like a miniature religious shrine. The vessel/shrine had been placed in one of the storerooms of a religious sanctuary shortly before the destruction of the city in about 1550 BCE. This type of icon was originally associated with Canaanite worship and later with the Israelite God Yahweh; it is perhaps best known from the biblical story of the golden calf and the Israelites at Mount Sinai (Exod. 32:4). Obviously the silver calf from Ashkelon is not the same as the golden calf from the Bible, but it was found in a religious context at the site and does indicate that such icons, or idols, were worshipped in the region during the Canaanite period, before the coming of the Israelites.

The Ashkelon excavation team also contributed unexpectedly to the quality of life for other foreign archaeologists working in Israel. The team members were housed in a five-star hotel for the early years of the dig, which represented a dramatic change in living conditions for the volunteers and staff, much to the envy of those participating in other excavations ongoing in the country at the time. Until that point, most excavations had housed their people in tents or in schools that were vacant for the summer; the staff and volunteers slept on cots, ate bad food, and shared toilets and showers with little room for privacy. The excavations at Ashkelon changed all that; as a result, today most foreign archaeological teams are based at either kibbutzim or hotels, with air-conditioned rooms in which to sleep and swimming pools in which to relax during down time. It may not sound important, but the contribution to archaeology was immeasurable—good food, a cold room, and decent showers can make a world of difference when spending much of the day excavating in the hot sun, with temperatures routinely more than 100 degrees.

Stager's excavations at Ashkelon were perhaps unique at the time in being funded essentially single-handedly by one private foundation, an unusual situation and one regarded with some envy by the other excavations. However, the practice has reemerged in the new millennium, with some archaeologists warning darkly that religious or political motivations on the part of the sponsors may unduly influence interpretation of the data, much as Sir Charles Marston's sponsorship of John Garstang's excavations at Jericho may have played a role in Garstang's fateful ascription of the destruction of the city to Joshua. For example, Eilat Mazar's sponsored excavations in Jerusalem on land owned by the 'Ir David (Elad) Foundation have been called into question, with the foundation accused by some of having political motives in sponsoring her excavations, namely a desire to claim a Jewish link to the past history of the area and establish more of a Jewish presence in the Silwan neighborhood of Jerusalem, just outside the walls of the Old City.

Chapter 6
The 1990s and beyond: from nihilism to the present

The early 1990s began with another attack on the discipline of biblical archaeology, not by William Dever this time but by a group of scholars known collectively as biblical minimalists. These scholars, who include Niels Peter Lemche, Thomas Thompson, Keith Whitelam, and Philip Davies, suggest that much of the Hebrew Bible and the history of ancient Israel is essentially a fabrication by writers and scholars living in either the Persian period in the fifth century BCE or the Hellenistic period in the third through first centuries BCE. They are called minimalists because they believe that the amount of actual history and historical facts contained in the Bible is minimal. The minimalists are frequently referred to as the Copenhagen School because several of them teach at the University of Copenhagen, although others are at the University of Sheffield in England. One should be aware that on the other side of the spectrum are the so-called biblical maximalists who argue that the biblical stories are indeed both completely factual and historically correct, even if they cannot always be verified by archaeology.

The minimalists have frequently attempted to use archaeology to strengthen their arguments. However, not one of them is a practicing field archaeologist, and their efforts sometimes backfire. The most famous example is that of the Tel Dan Stele. The first fragment of the stele was found in 1993 at the site of the same name, located in northern Israel near the modern Lebanese border and the headwaters of the Jordan River. The site has been continuously excavated since 1966 by teams led first by Avraham Biran and now by David Ilan of the Hebrew Union College-Jewish Institute of Religion in Jerusalem. On the Tel Dan Stele is the earliest extrabiblical inscription ever found that documents the existence of the House of David (*Beit David*). It was discovered just as a debate concerning whether David and Solomon had ever existed was reaching a crescendo among scholars. At a single blow, the finding of this inscription brought an end to the debate and settled the question of whether David was an actual historical person.

As it is currently reconstructed, the inscription describes the defeat of both Joram, king of Israel, and Ahaziyahu, king of Judah, by a king of Aram-Damascus in the ninth century BCE. It reads in part:

Now the king of Israel entered formerly in the land in my father's land; [but] Hadad made me myself king, and Hadad went in front of me; [and] I departed from [the] seven [...] of my kingdom; and I slew seve[nty ki]ngs, who harnessed thou[sands of cha]riots and thousands of horsemen. [And I killed Jo]ram, son of A[hab,] king of Israel, and [I] killed [Ahazi]yahu, son of [Joram, kin]g of the House of David; and I set [their towns into ruins ? ... the ci]ties of their land into de[solation ? ...] ... other and to overturn all their cities ? ... and Jehu] [ru]led over Is[rael ...] siege upon [...]

Gila Cook, the expedition's surveyor, discovered the first fragment from the stele. She had gone out to the site in the early afternoon and happened to notice that one of the rocks in a wall that had recently been excavated had letters inscribed upon it. It seems that the original inscription, which had been inscribed and erected at Tel Dan in about 842 BCE, had later been taken down and broken into fragments, some of which were eventually reused in the wall. It was only because of the raking light of the afternoon sun that she could see the inscribed letters, which had been missed by all previous members of the excavation team, including the volunteers who had excavated the wall of which the stone was now a part. Two more fragments came to light the following summer, in 1994, and the three fragments now form what is left of the Tel Dan Stele. It is possible that more will be found in the future.

The finding of the inscription caused a major sensation and was published on the front page of the *New York Times* and in *Time* magazine. It continued to make news when Niels Peter Lemche, one of the most prominent members of the Copenhagen School, suggested that the inscription might be a forgery planted by the excavator, Avraham Biran. However, Biran was one of the oldest, most distinguished, and most trusted archaeologists working in the state of Israel—he was Albright's first PhD student at Johns Hopkins University and the longtime director of the Nelson Glueck School of Biblical Archaeology at the Hebrew Union College-Jewish Institute of Religion in Jerusalem—and no serious scholar doubted the authenticity of the fragments. Nor did they question the interpretation of the inscription when other minimalists suggested that *Beit David* might not mean the "House of David" but something else entirely (such as the word "house" connected with the word "beloved," "uncle," or "kettle"). Today, after much further discussion in academic journals, it is accepted by most archaeologists that the inscription is not only genuine but that the reference is indeed to the House of David, thus representing the first allusion found anywhere outside the Bible to the biblical David.

In 1996, undeterred by the skepticism with which his Tel Dan Stele forgery hypothesis had been greeted, Niels Peter Lemche claimed that another inscription, which had just been found at the site of Tel Miqne some twenty-three miles southwest of Jerusalem, was also a forgery. Lemche's accusation was eventually dismissed, and the so-called Tel Miqne/Ekron Inscription has been recognized by virtually all other scholars as another important discovery for biblical archaeology.

Tel Miqne, the site excavated by Trude Dothan and Sy Gitin from 1981 to 1996, had first been tentatively identified in 1957 by Joseph Naveh of the Hebrew University of Jerusalem as Ekron, one of the five capital cities of the Philistines mentioned frequently in the Bible (the others being Ashkelon, Ashdod, Gath, and Gaza). The inscription was found during the thirteenth and final season of excavation at the site, in an area known as Temple Complex 650. Discovered in a level dating to the time of the Neo-Babylonian king Nebuchadnezzar, who destroyed the site in 603 BCE, it confirmed Naveh's suggestion that Tel Miqne represented the archaeological remains of Ekron, for the inscription had apparently originally been commissioned by a king of Ekron named Achish to commemorate the construction of a temple in the city, probably sometime in the early seventh century BCE.

Written using a Phoenician script, the inscription reads as follows: "The temple (which) Achish, son of Padi, son of Ysd, son of 'Ada,' son of Ya'ir, ruler of Ekron, built for Ptnyh, his Lady. May she bless him, and keep him, and prolong his days, and bless his land." Achish and his father Padi, the first two kings mentioned in this inscription, are both known from other, Neo-Assyrian, inscriptions. The Neo-Assyrian king Sennacherib, who marched into Judah and wreaked havoc in 701 BCE while putting down the rebellion of Hezekiah of Jerusalem, recounts in one inscription that he forced Hezekiah to reinstate Padi as king of Ekron. Later kings of Assyria, namely Esarhaddon and Ashurbanipal, also commissioned inscriptions referring to "Ikausu, king of Ekron"—a reference to Achish.

The discovery of the Tel Miqne/Ekron Inscription represents one of the few times that an inscription has been found which definitively identifies an archaeological site with a specific ancient city. It is the type of discovery that most biblical archaeologists can only dream about.

Eventually, the debate about biblical minimalism, especially with regard to David and Solomon, their rule in Jerusalem, and the extent of their empires, spread—perhaps not surprisingly—to encompass the city of Jerusalem itself. By their time, the city was already some two thousand years old, so the specific archaeological argument concerned the size and wealth of the tenth century BCE city in particular. While some scholars argued that it was indeed a mighty capital city, as described by the Bible, others believed that it was simply a small "cow town." In fact, it is still not clear where David and Solomon are positioned along the continuum from tribal chieftains to mighty kings and just how large the city itself was during their time.

During her excavations in Jerusalem after 1961, Kathleen Kenyon had discovered the remains of what archaeologists call the Stepped Stone Structure in an area that is just outside the walls of the Old City. This is sometimes thought to be part of the defensive system erected by the Jebusites from whom David captured the city. More recently, excavations by Eilat Mazar of the Shalem Center in Jerusalem within this same area suggest that this Stepped Stone Structure may be connected to a much larger building. Her excavations uncovered massive walls, which she identified as the remains of a building that she called the "Large Stone Structure," and which she said was part of a complex that included the Stepped Stone Structure on the slope. She identifies this complex as the palace of King David, in part because of its location and the date of the associated pottery, which she regards as dating to the tenth century BCE.

However, it is by no means clear whether this is David's palace. Israel Finkelstein and three other archaeologists from Tel Aviv University argue that it is not. They assert, on the basis of construction techniques and structural differences, in addition to

8. The Stepped Stone Structure in Jerusalem, excavated by Kathleen Kenyon, is arguably her most important discovery in the city. It is usually thought to have been part of the original Jebusite (i.e., Canaanite) defensive system of the city, dating back to the Bronze Age.

pottery and other finds, that the walls unearthed by Mazar do not belong to a single building but rather to several, and that the pottery and other remains indicate that the Stepped Stone Structure represents at least two phases of construction—with the lower part possibly dating to the ninth century BCE and the upper part dating to the Hellenistic period.

Finkelstein has been a major player in recent discussions concerning the precise dating of both artifacts and events purportedly dating to the time of David and Solomon. Throughout the 1990s, Finkelstein proposed a re-dating of the traditional chronology—which places the dates of the reigns of David and Solomon in the tenth century BCE—and suggested instead that much of the pottery and other materials that had been dated to the tenth century BCE should in fact be assigned instead to the ninth century BCE.

Previously, Yigael Yadin was convinced he had found evidence for a "blueprint" of Solomonic activity at all three sites outside of

Jerusalem associated with Solomon in the Hebrew Bible—namely the gates and casemate walls built at Megiddo, Hazor, and Gezer. However, all of this architectural evidence has now been reconsidered as part of the larger debate concerning the nature of David and Solomon, and it has been suggested, by Finkelstein and others, that they may not date to the reign of Solomon but may instead have been built by a ruler who came after the time of Solomon, such as Ahab or Omri, or even by different rulers in Israel and Judah.

Finkelstein's proposed re-dating of these structures to the ninth century BCE comes not only from a suggested reexamination of the relevant pottery found during the excavations at these sites, but from radiocarbon dates that have recently become available. Measuring radiocarbon, or C^{14}, as it is known in the literature, is a process invented by the American chemist and Nobel Prize-winner Willard Libby in 1949. It has proven increasingly useful to archaeologists ever since and is one of the major technological advances to have affected biblical archaeology since 1950. It provides archaeologists with a date when specific organisms—whether humans, trees, plants, or animals—died or stopped growing, by measuring the amount of C^{14} still present in the excavated remains. It therefore suggests a date for the stratigraphical level or context at a site in which such remains are found. However, it cannot give a precise date (e.g., 1005 BCE); rather, it provides a statistical probability that the date falls within a given range of years (e.g., 1005 BCE $\pm$ 15 years = 1020–990 BCE).

However, Amihai Mazar, a distinguished archaeologist from the Hebrew University of Jerusalem and cousin of Eilat Mazar, takes the position that the traditional dating for David and Solomon—in the tenth century BCE—is correct, countering Finkelstein's arguments with radiocarbon dates from his own site of Tel Rehov, as well as other sites in Israel, among other data. As a result of this debate, two alternative versions of the archaeology and history of Israel from this time period are now available, but the debate remains unresolved, with the size and importance and correct dates of the kingdoms of David and Solomon hanging in the balance.

Finally, besides issues of chronology, biblical archaeology during the 1990s and into the new millennium closely followed trends seen elsewhere in world archaeology. Rather than continuing to excavate biblical sites without an explicit methodology beyond determining the history of the site, the leading practitioners began to ask specific questions designed to allow the investigation of topics such as ethnicity, migration, gender, feasting, the rise of rulership, and other anthropologically oriented themes. These questions in turn demand not only the utilization of traditional methods of excavation but the supplementation of such methods with hard science, such as DNA analysis, residue analysis, and petrography, which will almost certainly be a hallmark of biblical archaeology in its next phase.

For example, at Amihai Mazar's site of Tel Rehov, in Israel's Bet She'an Valley, thirty beehives (forming an apiary or bee yard) from the tenth or ninth century BCE were found. The beehives are the earliest discovered anywhere in the ancient Near East and give new meaning to the biblical phrase "land of milk and honey." The excavators had already begun to suspect that they were excavating an apiary, so they decided to employ residue analysis—in which the surface of an excavated vessel is scraped, or a small piece of it is crushed, and a gas chromatography instrument and mass spectroscopy are used to look for any organic materials that may indicate the type of food that was once contained in the vessel. At Rehov, the residue analysis indicated the presence of degraded beeswax in the vessels, confirming the archaeologists' suspicions that they were indeed excavating an apiary.

By the turn of the new millennium, biblical archaeologists were also using advanced detection techniques such as magnetometers, ground-penetrating radar, electric resistivity meters, and satellite photography alongside traditional methods of excavation. These techniques enable archaeologists to peer beneath the ground surface before physical excavation begins. Outlines of walls and other physical features, including monumental gates to cities such as Megiddo, can be seen before a pickaxe ever touches the soil, thus allowing archaeologists to use their precious resources in predetermined areas that will produce useful results.

For instance, in 2003 archaeologist Assaf Yasur-Landau and geophysicist Yizhaq Makovsky from Tel Aviv University joined forces temporarily and revisited the site of Tel Kabri, which had previously been excavated from 1986 to 1993. The earlier excavators, Israeli archaeologist Aharon Kempinski and German archaeologist Wolf-Dietrich Niemeier, had uncovered a Canaanite palace at the site dating to the Middle Bronze Age, just after the time of Abraham. Yasur-Landau and Makovsky were wondering if perhaps the palace might not have been even larger than Kempinski and Niemeier had suspected. They employed two methods of detection, electric resistivity (or conductivity) and magnetometry, without ever breaking out a pick or a trowel.

Both methods are used to detect walls and other architectural features buried below ground. Magnetometers measure the strength of the local magnetic field—in addition to the earth's magnetic field, some archaeological features have a measurable magnetic field. For instance, if there is a buried ditch in the area, the soil within the ditch will frequently contain magnetic particles, which can be measured and which will show up differently on the sensor than a part of the site without a buried ditch. Similarly, a resistivity meter—which usually consists of two metal spikes inserted into the ground and attached by wires to a electric box—will measure the amount of resistance to an electrical current passing through the ground: the wetter the soil, the lower the resistance. If there is a buried stone wall or a hard pavement present below ground, such features will show up because of their resistance to conducting the electrical current.

At Tel Kabri, both methods indicated the presence of buried walls in an area of the site immediately adjacent to that in which the earlier excavations had found the remains of the Middle Bronze Age Canaanite palace. When preliminary excavations were subsequently undertaken by Yasur-Landau and the present author in 2005, it was confirmed that the palace was twice as large as the previous excavators had imagined, with both stone walls and solid plaster floors found about six feet beneath the present ground level. As a result, a new series of excavations was initiated at the site. Similar remote sensing detection systems are now being used with good results at other sites in the Holy Land and elsewhere, initiating a new phase in archaeology that holds great promise for the future.

Part II
Archaeology and the Bible

Chapter 7
From Noah and the Flood to Joshua and the Israelites

While biblical archaeologists working today are generally more interested in learning about details of daily life in the ancient biblical world than proving or disproving the accounts in the Bible, many lay people have these priorities reversed. They want to know: Did the Flood take place? Did Abraham and the Patriarchs exist? Were Sodom and Gomorrah destroyed by fire and brimstone? Did the Exodus occur? These were some of the original questions in biblical archaeology that intrigued the earliest pioneers of the field. They still resonate today but are far from being answered by biblical archaeologists.

In fact, solutions and answers to such questions are more frequently proposed by pseudo-archaeologists or archaeological charlatans, who take the public's money to support ventures that offer little chance of furthering the cause of knowledge. Every year, "scientific" expeditions embark to look for the Garden of Eden, Noah's Ark, Sodom and Gomorrah, the Ark of the Covenant, and the Ten Lost Tribes of Israel. These expeditions are often supported by prodigious sums of money donated by gullible believers who eagerly accept tales spun by sincere but misguided amateurs or by rapacious confidence men.

These ventures, which usually originate outside the confines of established scholarly institutions, engender confusion about what is real and what is fake. By practicing pseudo-archaeology rather than by using established archaeological principles and real science, the archaeological charlatans bring discredit to the field of biblical archaeology.

The fact of the matter is that during the past one hundred or so years, there have been fabulous archaeological discoveries in the Near East of sites dating from the second millennium BCE. However, while these have provided enormous insights into the Canaanites of Syro-Palestine, the Hittites of Anatolia, the Egyptians, and the peoples of Mesopotamia, all of whom are relevant to the biblical text and to the world of the Bible, such discoveries have shed relatively little light on the actual stories found in the Hebrew Bible—particularly those in Genesis and Exodus. As a result, many of the earlier stories in the Hebrew Bible, especially those from Creation to the Exodus, have not been corroborated by archaeologists and remain a matter of faith.

On the other hand, events from a slightly later period, i.e., during the era of the Divided Kingdoms in the first millennium BCE after the empire of David and Solomon broke asunder, benefit from extrabiblical inscriptions, records, and other data that can be used to corroborate the biblical details. For instance, the attack on Judah in 701 BCE by Sennacherib and the Neo-Assyrians and the destruction of Jerusalem and the Temple in 586 BCE by Nebuchadnezzar and the Neo-Babylonians are events described in the Hebrew Bible that have been independently confirmed by archaeological excavation and artifacts.

A good example of the difficulties involved in finding archaeological evidence for events depicted in the early portions of the Hebrew Bible, and for the opportunities that this provides to the pseudo-archaeologists is that of the Flood and Noah's Ark, as described in the book of Genesis.

In 1929, the British archaeologist Leonard Woolley—who had, fifteen years earlier, partnered with T. E. Lawrence in conducting an archaeological survey of the Negev—was excavating at the ancient site of Kish, in what is now modern Iraq, when he and his team came upon several feet of silt that had been laid down by a flood in antiquity. Both below and above the silt were man-made artifacts, including pottery, demonstrating that humans had lived at the site before and after the flood. It was Woolley's wife who excitedly exclaimed that he had "found the Flood!" The discovery made headlines in newspapers around the world, but within a short time Woolley disavowed any such connection, stating that what he had found was simply evidence for a local flood, rather than a worldwide inundation. In fact, evidence for such local floods has been found at a number of sites in Mesopotamia, which is not surprising since this is the "land between two rivers"—namely the Tigris and Euphrates rivers, which frequently overflowed their banks and flooded nearby areas.

On a larger scale, there is geological evidence that in the not too distant past, certainly by the time that humans occupied areas of the Near East and Asia Minor, extensive flooding sometimes occurred over a wider area. In 1997, William Ryan and Walter Pitman, two geologists at Columbia University, presented data documenting such an event in the area of the Black Sea around 7,500 years ago, when the sea broke through its barriers and flooded a large area in Turkey and perhaps farther south. These events could have been the catalysts for myths and epics of a great flood.

It is conceivable that such localized, perhaps devastating, floods were the origin for the stories told by the Sumerians, Akkadians, and Babylonians that have so many details in common with the story of Noah and his Ark in the Hebrew Bible. The first such story appears to be a Sumerian version, perhaps dating back to about 2700 BCE, featuring a man named Ziusudra who survives the Flood. In a version dating to several hundred years later, the survivor is a man named Atrahasis. By 1800 BCE, in the Epic of Gilgamesh, it is Utnapishtim who survives the Flood and tells the story to the epic's protagonist, Gilgamesh. Only much later, most likely sometime between 1200 and 900 BCE, was the biblical version of Noah and the Flood written down.

The details of these stories are too close to be coincidental. In essence, these versions seem to originate from the same story, although some of the details differ—the name of the Flood survivor, the number and types of birds released immediately after the Flood, and the reasons behind the inundation. In the earlier versions, for example, the flood is sent because humans are too noisy; in the biblical version it is sent because humans are too evil and corrupt. The biblical story of the Flood may therefore be an example of a "transmitted narrative"—a story that is not only handed down from generation to generation within a tribe or people but from culture to culture as well, as from the Sumerians to Akkadians to Babylonians, and then to the Israelites, perhaps via the Canaanites.

However, in terms of archaeology, no indisputable evidence for a worldwide flood has yet been uncovered by archaeologists. Similarly, no remains of Noah's Ark have yet been found by a credible professional archaeologist. And yet, claims are made almost every year that another "expedition" has found the Ark. A prime example is Bob Cornuke, founder of the Bible Archaeology Search and Exploration (BASE) Institute in Colorado. Cornuke is a self-described former police investigator and SWAT team member turned biblical investigator, international explorer, and best-selling author.

In 2006 Cornuke led an expedition searching for Noah's Ark. Some media reports announced that Cornuke's team had discovered boat-shaped rocks at an altitude of 13,000 feet on Mount Suleiman in Iran's Elburz mountain range. Cornuke said the rocks look "uncannily like wood.... We have had [cut] thin sections of the rock made, and we can see [wood] cell structures." But peer review by professional geologists quickly debunked these findings. Kevin Pickering, a geologist at University College London who specializes in sedimentary rocks, said, "The photos appear to show iron-stained sedimentary rocks, probably thin beds of silicified sandstones and shales, which were most likely laid down in a marine environment a long time ago." Despite the grandstanding by Cornuke, there was no archaeological—or geological—evidence that the Ark had been located.

Among the many sites at which Leonard Woolley excavated was a site in Mesopotamia known as Tell Muqayyar. According to inscriptions found at Tell Muqayyar itself, it was the site of an ancient city named Ur. Woolley and others quickly linked this site to the biblical "Ur of the Chaldees"—according to tradition, the birthplace of Abraham, the patriarch revered in Judaism, Christianity, and Islam. However, there were several sites in the ancient Near East that had the name Ur, just as there are many cities and towns in the United States today with the name "Troy," and it is not clear which city named Ur, if any, is to be associated with Abraham, just as none of the cities in the United States are actually associated with the original Trojan War.

The question of the existence of Abraham, Isaac, and Jacob—the Patriarchs, as they are called—remains a contentious issue among archaeologists and biblical scholars. While some archaeologists argue that the details contained in the stories of the Patriarchs and their wanderings fit well within the conditions and practices of the early second millennium BCE, others argue that the stories and the characters could just as easily have been made up centuries later, in the first millennium BCE. The simple fact of the matter is that although numerous excavations have recovered tremendous quantities of archaeological remains from the early second through the early first millennia BCE, at sites in lands ranging from ancient Mesopotamia to Canaan to Egypt, there has not yet been any direct

archaeological or extrabiblical textual evidence found to confirm or
deny the existence of Abraham and his fellow Patriarchs.

Similarly, perhaps the most vexing question asked by, and most
frequently of, biblical archaeologists, is whether there is evidence
that the Exodus took place. Exodus with a capital "E" refers to the
departure of the Hebrews from Egypt, where they had been
enslaved by a succession of pharaohs. Acknowledgment of that
event (or at least a portion of it) is celebrated annually by the
Jewish festival of Passover. However, despite attempts by a
number of biblical archaeologists—and an even larger number of
amateur enthusiasts—over many years, credible direct
archaeological evidence for the Exodus has yet to be found. While it
can be argued that such evidence would be difficult to find, since
nomads generally do not leave behind permanent installations,
archaeologists have discovered and excavated nomadic
emplacements from other periods in the Sinai desert. So if there
were archaeological remains to be found from the Exodus, one
would have expected them to be found by now. And yet, thus far
there is no trace of the biblical "600,000 men on foot, besides
children" plus "a mixed crowd...and livestock in great numbers"
(Exod. 12:37–38) who wandered for forty years in the desert. That
is not to say that such an event did not take place, but merely that
no archaeological evidence has yet been found for it.

Related to the Exodus story is the biblical account regarding the
Israelite conquest of Canaan, which is told in the books of Judges
and Joshua in the Hebrew Bible. It describes how Joshua and his
army swept down upon the land and overran it in a lightning series
of attacks, destroying the major Canaanite cities and capturing
their kings. Over the past century, biblical archaeologists have
argued about when this took place—settling upon 1250 BCE as the
most likely time because of Pharaoh Merneptah's inscription of
1207 BCE that mentions an entity named "Israel" in the region of
Canaan by that date—and have suggested several competing
theories concerning how the Israelite conquest of Canaan actually

took place, based upon the archaeological evidence discovered during excavations at the various sites named in the biblical account.

For instance, William F. Albright favored the Conquest Model, which took the biblical account of events essentially at face value, arguing that the conquest occurred after a sudden and violent blitzkrieg attack. Not everyone agreed. Two German scholars, Albrecht Alt and Martin Noth, favored a Peaceful Infiltration Model, suggesting that over time small groups of Hebrew nomads entered Canaan quietly. Americans George Mendenhall and Norman Gottwald suggested the Revolting Peasants Model, arguing that the Israelites were an underclass within Canaanite society and that the conquest was actually a Marxist-type rebellion in which the oppressive upper class was overthrown and the proletariat took over. And finally, Israel Finkelstein has suggested the Invisible Israelites Model, which argues that Israelites and Canaanites were both present and sharing the land until the economy of Canaan collapsed following the withdrawal of Egypt from the region at the end of the Late Bronze Age. At that time, and only then, the Israelites gradually, and peacefully, emerged from the shadow of the Canaanites and took over.

All of these models call upon archaeological evidence to support their arguments. There is a small problem, however, for those who would follow Albright and the Conquest Model. Many of the sites mentioned in the biblical account and specifically noted as being destroyed by the invading Israelites have now been excavated by biblical archaeologists, with an interesting conundrum resulting. On the one hand, most of the sites described as being destroyed do not show any archaeological evidence of destruction—and some, such as Jericho, were not even occupied at the time. On the other hand, there are sites in the region that were definitely destroyed at that time, but none of these sites is mentioned in the biblical account. One of the few places named in the Bible as being destroyed by the Israelites and at which a destruction has been found by archaeologists is the site of Hazor.

In fact, Yigael Yadin believed that his excavations at Hazor in the 1950s had found evidence for the Israelite destruction of the thirteenth-century BCE city established at the site, thus confirming (for him) the biblical account of the Israelite conquest of Canaan. After a break of more than three decades, excavations at Hazor began again in 1990, directed by Yadin's former student Amnon Ben-Tor, who found additional remains from this destroyed city. There is still debate as to who was responsible for the destruction— was it Israelites, Egyptians, Canaanites, or Sea Peoples?

Like Yadin before him, Ben-Tor argues that the Israelites are the most likely perpetrators of this destruction and provides a list of reasons why this is so, including the fact that neither the Egyptians nor the Canaanites were guilty because both Egyptian and Canaanite statues were found defiled in the destruction level, and neither group would have condoned such an act. But not all scholars are convinced by his arguments, and it is difficult to decide between Israelites, a destructive migrating group known as the Sea Peoples who appeared in the region at about the same time, or some other unknown group as the agents of destruction at Hazor. There is no archaeological evidence that contradicts Yadin's and Ben-Tor's theory, but there is also no additional archaeological evidence to support it at the moment.

Important components of this discussion are the related questions of who, exactly, the Israelites were and how one knows when one has uncovered archaeological evidence for their existence. It used to be an accepted axiom in biblical archaeology that if one found collar-rim jars or four-room houses in a Late Bronze Age or Early Iron Age settlement, then one was excavating an Israelite settlement, since those items were considered to be uniquely Israelite and not Canaanite in origin. More recently, though, a number of scholars have stated that such objects and structures are not unique to the Israelites and, indeed, may not be unique to the Early Iron Age.

So, how does one tell an Israelite from a Canaanite? It has been suggested by some archaeologists that an absence of pig bones from a settlement of the appropriate time period may be an indication of the presence of Israelites, rather than Canaanites, because of the prohibitions against eating pork set out in the Hebrew Bible. Others insist that one cannot make such a generalized observation and that, in any event, arguing from negative evidence—the lack or absence of something at a site—is always dangerous since the next trowelful of dirt may turn up the necessary piece of evidence. The question, like many others in biblical archaeology, remains open.

Chapter 8

From David and Solomon to Nebuchadnezzar and the Neo-Babylonians

Debates concerning David and Solomon have been at the forefront of biblical archaeology for a long time, but especially since the early 1990s when their very existence was called into question. The problem is that although the Tel Dan Stele—fragments of which were discovered in 1993 and 1994—now presents us with the first known extrabiblical attestation for the House of David (*Beit David*), there is little other direct archaeological evidence available for either king at the moment.

On the other hand, biblical archaeologists have had considerably more success in corroborating the biblical accounts concerned with events just after the time of David and Solomon, during the early first millennium BCE from ca. 925 BCE to 586 BCE. There are extrabiblical inscriptions, archival and accounting records, and other data from this period, including inscriptions that name individual kings of Israel and Judah, archaeological evidence of Sennacherib's attack on Judah in 701 BCE, and Nebuchadnezzar's destruction of Jerusalem and the Temple in 586 BCE. In a certain sense, it is fortunate that military destruction sometimes leaves an archaeological record that can be correlated with biblical texts.

According to the biblical account, one of the first major events to take place after the death of Solomon was an invasion by Pharaoh

Shishak of Egypt in about 925 BCE. According to the text (1 Kings 14.25; 2 Chron. 12.9), Shishak invaded the land of Judah and besieged the city of Jerusalem, carrying away "the treasures of the house of the LORD." Egyptologists have long noted the existence of an inscription written on the walls of the Temple of Amon in Karnak (modern Luxor), recording an attack made by a Pharaoh Sheshonq upon the region of Israel and Judah, with a list of 150 cities that he claimed to have conquered. Sheshonq was the founder of the Twenty-second Dynasty of Egypt, coming to the throne ca. 945 BCE and ruling until ca. 924 BCE.

Among the conquered cities listed by Sheshonq was Megiddo. And at Megiddo itself, the Chicago excavators in 1925 recovered a fragment from a stone inscription bearing the royal cartouche of Sheshonq. It came from the type of inscription usually reserved for use by the Egyptians as a victory monument placed at a site that they had captured and then occupied. The inscription had later been broken up, with the pieces reused as building material. The fragment had been uncovered during the 1903–1905 excavations at Megiddo by Schumacher, but had been thrown out on the spoil heap, where it was later discovered by the Chicago workmen. Sheshonq's claim to have captured Megiddo was thus corroborated archaeologically. However, it remains unresolved whether the Egyptian Sheshonq is the same as the biblical Shishak, although most archaeologists and biblical scholars believe this to be the case.

Sheshonq's attack took advantage of the fact that the United Monarchy of David and Solomon had split into the two separate kingdoms of Israel and Judah immediately after the death of Solomon. Many stories in the Hebrew Bible concern kings who ruled the lands during this period of the Divided Kingdoms. Several of these kings are mentioned in Neo-Assyrian and Neo-Babylonian texts from the early first millennium BCE, thus providing independent corroboration for their historical existence. One can speculate that if the kings in the Bible are real, then its various descriptions of daily life may well be accurate too.

One northern king discussed by the biblical writers is Ahab, son of Omri, who married Jezebel and who "did evil in the sight of the LORD more than all who were before him" (1 Kings 16:30). The Bible recounts a number of battles that Ahab fought against Ben-Hadad of Aram who ruled from Damascus (as 1 Kings 20 says). Ahab is mentioned in an extrabiblical inscription on a seven-foot-tall stone monument that dates to 853 BCE. This, the so-called Monolith Inscription of the Neo-Assyrian king Shalmaneser III, describes a battle that he fought at the city of Karkar, located in what is now modern Syria. There Shalmaneser fought against a coalition of troops gathered from Damascus, Bylos, Egypt, Israel, and elsewhere, including 2,000 chariots and 10,000 infantry belonging to Ahab:

> Karkar, his royal city, I destroyed, I devastated, I burned with fire. 1,200 chariots, 1,200 cavalry, 20,000 soldiers, of Hadad-ezer, of Aram; 700 chariots, 700 cavalry, 10,000 soldiers of Irhuleni of Hamath; 2,000 chariots, 10,000 soldiers of Ahab, the Israelite ... — these twelve kings he brought to his support; to offer battle and fight, they came against me.

Some archaeologists and historians have suggested that the Ben-Hadad mentioned in the Bible as Ahab's enemy and the Hadad-ezer described in Shalmaneser's inscription as Ahab's ally are one and the same person, but this theory is still unsupported by hard evidence. We can say with relative confidence, however, that Shalmaneser's text clearly establishes that Ahab was a real, historical person. Moreover, excavations conducted during the 1990s by Israeli archaeologist David Ussishkin and British archaeologist John Woodhead at the site of ancient Jezreel, which was located near Megiddo and was the home city to Ahab and his wife Jezebel according to the biblical account, confirms that there was indeed a city in existence at the site during the appropriate time period, i.e., the ninth century BCE. Unfortunately, thus far even the most ardent of archaeological investigators have been unable to find confirmatory evidence that Jezebel was actually thrown out of a window and eaten by dogs (2 Kings 9:30–37).

Archaeological evidence also exists to confirm that King Jehu was a real person. The biblical account (2 Kings 8:25–10:27) relates that Jehu usurped the throne of Israel by killing both the king of Israel and the king of Judah. Jehu is independently described as the "son of Omri" (to whom he may or may not have actually been related) on the so-called Black Obelisk—another seven-foot-tall stone monument of Shalmaneser III—dating to 841 BCE. Jehu is depicted there, bowing at the feet of the king. The accompanying text reads: "Tribute of Iaua (Jehu), son of Omri. Silver, gold, a golden bowl, a golden beaker, golden goblets, pitchers of gold, lead, staves (staffs) for the hand of the king, javelins, I received from him."

Almost 150 years later, the Neo-Assyrian King Sennacherib invaded the land of Judah and marched on Jerusalem in 701 BCE—an event recorded in the Bible. His forces attacked forty-six cities, including the second-largest in the land, Lachish. The biblical account states succinctly: "In the fourteenth year of King Hezekiah, King Sennacherib of Assyria came up against all the fortified cities of Judah and captured them" (2 Kings 18:13).

This event was extensively confirmed by major archaeological excavations at the site of Lachish, conducted by David Ussishkin of Tel Aviv University beginning in 1973. Lachish was the focus of earlier excavations by James L. Starkey, from 1932 to 1938, but those ended when Starkey was murdered while traveling to Jerusalem for the opening of the Palestine Archaeological Museum (now called the Rockefeller Museum), in East Jerusalem. Ussishkin realized that the "tons and tons" of rocks and stones that Starkey and his team had been trying to dig through were actually the remnants of a siege ramp that the Neo-Assyrians had built when they attacked the city in 701 BCE. In addition, he found a Judean countersiege ramp within the city dating to the same period.

The site of Lachish is inextricably and forever linked to Jerusalem because of passages found in the Hebrew Bible and in extrabiblical depictions and inscriptions at the ancient site of Nineveh in what is now Iraq. Its importance for biblical archaeology lies not only in its connections to the Bible but in the careful and deliberate way that it was stratigraphically excavated by Ussishkin, and in the means by which he was able to use a variety of different sources, from as far away as Nineveh, to establish the history of the site. Ussishkin published the results of his excavations in a mammoth set of five volumes containing all the data uncovered by the expedition, from macroscopic architectural details to microscopic details of archaeobotany in each phase of the city's history.

When Sennacherib and his men eventually captured Lachish, they marched the captives back to Assyria—part of the more than 200,000 Judean exiles that Sennacherib claims to have deported in this campaign. Sennacherib ordered pictures of his triumph to be engraved and displayed on the walls of a room in his "Palace without a Rival," as he called it, at Nineveh in Assyria, on the banks of the Euphrates.

These pictures, which one can follow like a modern cartoon strip in panels along the four walls of the room, depict the entire siege. First, the Assyrian warriors, archers, and infantrymen march up to the city. Then the siege engines are wheeled up the seven or more ramps that the Assyrians built (including the one excavated by Starkey and then Ussishkin). Next is the battle for the city itself, with torches flying through the air and the defenders shooting arrows from the defensive towers, and then the aftermath, with triumphant Assyrians carrying away loot as some of the defeated Judeans are staked out on the ground and flayed alive, while others have their heads cut off (which are then hung from trees and used for target practice by Assyrians). The vast majority of the Jews are depicted as refugees, trudging toward far-off Assyria with their families and their belongings stacked on carts. Sennacherib himself is shown in one of the final scenes, seated on his throne as goods and captives are presented before him.

The depiction of the siege and capture of Lachish in Sennacherib's palace at Nineveh was undoubtedly meant not only to immortalize the victory but also to serve as propaganda. It was a warning to the ambassadors and visiting delegations from other subservient nations not to rebel against the might of Assyria. It was effective, for though the Neo-Assyrians seem to have been as brutal and bloodthirsty as they depicted themselves, they apparently negotiated diplomatic settlements as often as they settled things on the battlefield.

The excavations by Starkey and then Ussishkin at Lachish, the depictions at Sennacherib's palace in Nineveh, and Sennacherib's own inscriptions offer separate and unique sources of information and evidence for the Neo-Assyrian siege of Lachish, a compelling corroboration and elaboration of the spare details that are given in the Hebrew Bible. This is one of the very few instances where there are numerous separate sources of evidence for an event in ancient Israel or Judah. For this reason, the discoveries relating to the Neo-Assyrian siege of Lachish in 701 BCE are considered to rank among the greatest finds to date in biblical archaeology.

After his successful capture of Lachish, Sennacherib and his army headed for Jerusalem. The Judean king Hezekiah laid in supplies and established a number of defensive mechanisms, or so it is written in the Hebrew Bible (2 Chron. 32 and Isa. 22:10). According to archaeologists, these defensive mechanisms may have included the construction of a wall more than 20 feet thick and 130 feet in length, for the Israeli archaeologist Nahman Avigad found a long segment of just such a wall (the so-called Broad Wall) in the Jewish Quarter of Jerusalem in the 1970s.

From the biblical account, it is unclear whether the defensive measures taken by Hezekiah actually succeeded, for two different tales are presented within the Hebrew Bible. In one instance (2 Kings 19:32–36; repeated, with slight differences, in Isa. 37:33–37 and 2 Chron. 32:20–21), the Bible says that a plague ravaged the Assyrian troops besieging the city, so that 185,000 died in a single night and the Assyrians subsequently retreated. However, in another instance (2 Kings 18:14–16), the biblical account states that Hezekiah sent a bribe to Sennacherib, who was still besieging Lachish at the time, to leave Jerusalem in peace, paying him three hundred talents of silver and thirty talents of gold.

Sennacherib's own records seem to corroborate the latter story, for in one of his inscriptions he records that a bribe was paid, but that it was in fact eight hundred talents of silver and thirty of gold. Moreover, he stated: "As for Hezekiah, the Judaean, he did not submit to my yoke. I laid siege to forty-six of his strong fortified cities, and countless small villages in their vicinity, and conquered them . . . I brought out of them 200,150 people, young and old, male and female, horses, mules, donkeys, camels, big and small cattle beyond counting, and considered them booty. Himself [Hezekiah] I shut up as a prisoner within Jerusalem, his royal residence, like a bird in a cage" (Oriental Institute Prism).

A little more than one hundred years later, Nebuchadnezzar and the Neo-Babylonians—successors to the Neo-Assyrians—attacked Jerusalem and captured the city in 597 and again in 586 BCE. The biblical account states, "Against him [King Jehoiakim of Judah] came up Nebuchadnezzar king of Babylon, and bound him in fetters to take him to Babylon" (2 Chron. 36:6). Elsewhere it states, "In his days, Nebuchadnezzar king of Babylon came up . . . and the Lord sent against him [Jehoiakim] bands of the Chaldeans [Neo-Babylonians] . . . and sent them against Judah to destroy it" (2 Kings 24:1–2).

These accounts are substantiated by an entry for the seventh year of Nebuchadnezzar's reign, found in the Babylonian Chronicles— contemporary records kept on clay tablets in Mesopotamia by the Neo-Babylonian priests of the chief events for each year, which have been recovered and translated by archaeologists. The records state: "In the seventh year [598/597 BCE], the month of Kislev, the king of Akkad mustered his troops, marched to the Hatti-land, and encamped against [i.e., besieged] the city of Judah and on the second day of the month of Adar he seized the city and captured the king. He appointed there a king of his own choice, received its heavy tribute and sent [them] to Babylon" (Chronicles of the Chaldaean Kings).

In other words, Nebuchadnezzar's scribes stated that Jerusalem was conquered and the vanquished peoples of Judah were transported to Babylon in 597 BCE, thereby corroborating the biblical account. Nebuchadnezzar and his army did the same thing again in 586 BCE, as mentioned, and for this attack and destruction we have archaeological evidence, in the form of ash, arrowheads, and toppled stones found in the Jewish Quarter of Jerusalem by Israeli archaeologist Nahman Avigad, excavating in the years after 1967.

Although it is likely that Nebuchadnezzar carried off the Hebrew royalty and the leading citizens of Jerusalem, as the Bible says— and initiated the Babylonian Exile of the Jews, which was to last for approximately fifty years (586–538 BCE)—recent archaeological surveys have shown that the land of Judah was not completely emptied of its inhabitants. This is contrary to what had been previously thought based upon the biblical account. Although there was a grave demographic crisis, as Oded Lipschits of Tel Aviv University has phrased it, archaeological surveys have confirmed that upwards of 70 percent of the population remained on the land during the years following the conquest—that is, sites continued to be occupied and there was no widespread abandonment of cities, towns, or villages as might have been expected. The majority of those left behind were probably peasants and members of the lower classes, for the members of the upper classes had all been taken off to Babylon.

Overall, the relevant extrabiblical inscriptions represent crucial confirming evidence for archaeologists that the biblical account does contain accurate details concerning first millennium BCE people, places, and events. These inscriptions have confirmed the existence of various kings of Israel and Judah mentioned in the biblical account and, in some cases, have corroborated the entire biblical account—such as the conquest of Jerusalem by Nebuchadnezzar in 597 BCE. In no case has the biblical account of an event in the early first millennium BCE yet been shown by an extrabiblical inscription to be completely false.

Chapter 9

From the Silver Amulet Scrolls to the Dead Sea Scrolls

In 1979, Gabriel Barkay, then a professor at Tel Aviv University, was able to illuminate the biblical account from a unique perspective, while excavating a number of tombs in Jerusalem in an area overlooking the Hinnom Valley. The tombs are located at the site of Ketef Hinnom (the "Shoulder of Hinnom"), an Iron Age cemetery situated to the south of the King David Hotel and next to the Scottish Presbyterian Church of St. Andrew.

One of the tombs—actually a burial cave (Cave 24)—had multiple chambers. In one of the chambers (Room 25) were the remains of more than ninety-five individuals, along with more than one thousand objects. At least seven hundred of the objects were found in a single repository, left undisturbed for at least 2,500 years under one of the burial benches. Among 263 intact pots and other vessels, numerous gold objects, one hundred or more pieces of silver jewelry, arrowheads, and axeheads was a silver coin minted in the sixth century BCE on the Greek island of Kos. It is one of the earliest coins ever found in Israel, for coinage had only just been invented at the beginning of the seventh century BCE in Turkey.

Even more interesting were two small amulets, each consisting of a small rolled-up strip of silver: one approximately four inches long by one inch wide; the other approximately one and a half inches long by half an inch wide. It took three years of painstaking work at the Israel Museum before the strips were fully unrolled. When that was finally accomplished, it was apparent that they were inscribed with minuscule writing. One word on the longer inscription jumped out at Yaakov Meshorer, curator of numismatics at the Israel Museum: *YHWH*, the tetragrammaton for the Divine Name Yahweh (Lord). Later it was established that the same word, *YHWH*, was inscribed on the smaller piece as well.

The two inscriptions appeared to contain priestly blessings in Hebrew, similar to the Priestly Benediction found in the Bible in Numbers 6:24–26, which says: "The Lord bless you and keep you; the Lord make his face to shine upon you, and be gracious to you; the Lord lift up his countenance upon you, and give you peace" (NRSV).

However, it was still not clear exactly what was written on the two amulets, for the writing on them was nearly illegible, due to the ravages of time. It took the combined efforts of the members of the West Semitic Research Project at the University of Southern California, headed by Bruce and Kenneth Zuckerman, to tease out the full text of the inscriptions, using a combination of photographic and computer imaging techniques, including fiber-optic technology.

Eventually it became clear that the inscription on the smaller piece reads "May he/she be blessed by Yahweh, the warrior [or helper] and the rebuker of [E]vil: May Yahweh bless you, keep you. May Yahweh make his face shine upon you and grant you p[ea]ce." The inscription on the longer piece is similar, reading

> ...]YHW ... the grea[t ... who keeps] the covenant and [G]
> raciousness towards those who love [him] and those who keep [his
> commandments ... ...]. the Eternal? [...]. [the?] blessing more
> than any [sna]re and more than Evil. For redemption is in him. For

YHWH is our restorer [and] rock. May YHWH bles[s] you and
[may he] keep you. [May] YHWH make [his face] shine...

Barkay suggested that the two amulets may have been deposited
soon after the city's destruction by Nebuchadnezzar and the
Neo-Babylonians in 586 BCE, since most of the pottery and other
objects found associated with them date to just after this period.
It is, however, impossible to tell exactly how old the amulets are,
although the paleography—the script used in the inscriptions—
suggests that they were inscribed sometime during the seventh or
sixth centuries BCE. What is clear, though, is that they have a
singular importance, for they are the oldest biblical texts currently
extant. The fact that they so closely repeat what is said in today's
versions of the Hebrew Bible only adds to their importance.

It is noteworthy that the amulets were found in what was
essentially a routine, albeit very carefully conducted, excavation by
a traditional team of archaeologists and students. What makes
their story so compelling—in addition to their inscriptions—is the
manner in which sheer ingenuity coupled together with modern
technology enabled determined scholars to unroll the amulets and
study the inscriptions.

Similar ingenuity and modern technology are now being used on
the Dead Sea Scrolls, which William Albright once called the
greatest manuscript discovery of modern times. Found more than
sixty years ago, these scrolls, written mostly between the third
century BCE and the first century CE, are relevant to both Jews
and Christians. The initial discovery of these famous scrolls was
not made by archaeologists but by Bedouins, who sold them to
antiquities dealers.

According to the traditional account of the story, back in 1947
three young men from a local Bedouin tribe were watering their
sheep and goats in the harsh desert area near the western side of
the Dead Sea. One of them began idly tossing rocks at the mouth of

a cave high up on a cliff above him. One of the stones sailed through the cave entrance, and the young boy standing below heard a crash. With evening rapidly approaching, the boy made his way back to camp and told his two acquaintances what had happened. In the morning, they climbed the cliff and entered the cave, where they found pieces of a shattered jar and several intact jars. At least one of the jars contained several tightly wrapped leather scrolls. Disappointed that they had not found gold, the boys gathered up the scrolls and returned to their camp.

Sometime later, the boys rejoined the rest of their tribe and hung the scrolls from a tent pole until the tribe's wanderings brought them close to the town of Bethlehem. There they brought the scrolls to an antiquities dealer named Kando, who bought them thinking that if he could not sell them as antiquities he could always sell the leather to be made into sandals. Kando, in turn, contacted Professor Eliezer Sukenik of the Hebrew University of Jerusalem, who traveled down to Kando's shop in Bethlehem to examine the scrolls. Sukenik purchased the three scrolls that Kando offered him and returned to Jerusalem just hours before fighting broke out in the Israeli War for Independence. The scrolls proved to be extremely important. One was a copy—at least one thousand years older than any previously known copy—of the book of Isaiah from the Hebrew Bible. The second scroll, now known as the Thanksgiving Scroll, contained hymns of thanks. The third scroll, known as the War Scroll, described an apocalyptic war between the "Sons of Light" and the "Sons of Darkness."

Subsequently, four more scrolls appeared on the antiquities market. These were eventually purchased by Yigael Yadin, Eliezer Sukenik's son (who had taken a Hebrew name by this time), through an intermediary after he saw a classified advertisement for them in the *Wall Street Journal*. The discovery of these first Dead Sea Scrolls touched off a race between the archaeologists and the Bedouins to find more scrolls. In the end, primarily between the years 1947 and 1960, both intact scrolls and thousands of fragments were discovered in at least eleven different caves located in the cliffs along the northwest shore of the Dead Sea, behind the archaeological ruins of the site of Qumran. All told, more than eight hundred scrolls, both intact and fragmentary, were found in these caves, most dating between 200 BCE and 70 CE. Other scrolls, and material artifacts as well, including leather sandals and woven baskets, were found in other caves located farther away from this region, some dating to the later period of the Second Jewish (or Bar Kokhba) Rebellion from 132 to 135 BCE, but it is these more than eight hundred scrolls from the Qumran region that are most well known to the general public.

The discovery of the scrolls was only the beginning of the story, for although they had been recovered from the depths of the caves in which they had lain for nearly two thousand years, the scrolls in

9. The Dead Sea Scrolls caves, located in the hills behind Qumran on the shores of the Dead Sea, held more than eight hundred whole and fragmentary scrolls written primarily during the second century BCE through the first century CE. The scrolls contained both biblical and nonbiblical material, including virtually all the books of the Hebrew Bible.

their entirety were still far from being translated and published. In fact, while some of the scrolls were published very quickly, a logjam of unpublished material still existed as recently as the early 1990s, with a number of scrolls from Cave 4 still being studied by a small group of senior scholars who had been granted the publication rights decades earlier. Their work had been complicated by the fact that the scrolls from that cave had disintegrated into some 15,000 small fragments, essentially rendering their work similar to a jigsaw puzzle enthusiast trying to work on an unknown number of puzzles simultaneously and without the help of the puzzle-box cover pictures to aid reconstruction.

The delay in publication led to all sorts of outlandish conspiracy theories, including the accusation that the Vatican was suppressing publication of the scrolls because they contained texts that would undermine the very tenets of Christianity. Suffice it to say, there was no such conspiracy and no such texts within the Dead Sea Scrolls, as was revealed when the publication logjam was finally broken and the final volumes with photographs, translations, and analyses began to appear in the late 1990s. Work on the scrolls continues today with techniques such as infrared photography and fiber-optic technology being used to help read and reconstruct the most damaged of the fragments, especially by the same West Semitic Research Project team members who had worked on the Ketef Hinnom silver amulets. Eventually, high-resolution digital photographs of all the fragments will be placed on the Internet for all to see.

Excavations at the nearby site of Qumran, located in front of the caves in which the Dead Sea Scrolls were found, were first begun in the 1950s by Father Roland de Vaux, of the École Biblique et Archéologique Française. He believed that Qumran had been a monastery and that the monks who lived there had written the Dead Sea Scrolls. The scrolls themselves, he thought, were hidden by their owners in the caves behind the site when the Romans invaded the area in 68 CE, destroying the site and removing its inhabitants. The scrolls then remained undisturbed for the next two thousand years.

Later scholars and excavators of the site have frequently disagreed with de Vaux's conclusions, suggesting instead that the site served as either a Roman villa, or a place of pottery manufacture, or a fortress. They have argued over whether the inhabitants were Essenes, a Jewish religious group that flourished from the second century BCE to the first century CE, as the Roman historian Josephus seems to imply, or some other Jewish group such as the Sadducees or Pharisees. It is also a matter of debate as to whether the scrolls came from Jerusalem or other parts of Judaea and were later deposited in the area of Qumran.

Regardless of such academic discussions, it is clear that the Dead Sea Scrolls are an extremely important part of the history of both Judaism and Christianity. The biblical texts they contain are a millennium older than the oldest ones previously known, which date to ca. 900 CE and were found in 1896 in a synagogue in Cairo. They therefore provide insights into the textual history of the Hebrew Bible and how the texts evolved over time. It is clear, however, that they represent merely one of at least three versions of the Hebrew Bible in existence at that time (different versions were known in Babylon, Palestine, and Egypt), demonstrating how fluid the situation was before the Hebrew Bible was canonized in its present form.

The nonbiblical texts among the Dead Sea Scrolls are fascinating as well. For instance, documents detailing the precise rules of the community that wrote the Dead Sea Scrolls provide an example of one type of Judaism that was practiced in that era, including instructions and prohibitions about eating, drinking, and congregating, and recording the fact that the people who wrote the scrolls were waiting for an Armageddon and the coming of a messiah.

One of the scrolls is written on copper, found separated into two pieces in Cave 3. It took years before the scroll was able to be unrolled, using distinctly old-fashioned technology in the form of a metal lathe at the Manchester Institute of Technology in England. This was used to cut the scroll into small segments, which were then pieced back together again and read. The scroll turned out to contain directions to sixty-four different buried treasures consisting of gold, silver, and other precious objects. Despite repeated attempts, primarily by amateur archaeologists, not one of the treasures has ever been located. In part this is probably due to the vagueness of the instructions; for instance, the directions to the first treasure are given simply as: "In the ruin which is in the valley, pass under the steps leading to the East forty cubits... there is a chest of money and its total [is] the weight of seventeen talents."

It is unclear what these treasures represent, if they even existed in the first place. If the scroll does reflect reality, then most likely they either were precious objects from the treasury of the Second Temple in Jerusalem, which had been hidden at the outbreak of the First Jewish Revolt in 66 CE, or were the annual tithes that had been destined for the Temple but which could not be brought to it because of the ongoing rebellion. Alternatively, the scroll may not reflect reality, but if that is the case, then one wonders at the reason for its existence.

Taken as a whole, the Dead Sea Scrolls contain copies—and in some cases multiple copies—of every book in the Hebrew Bible except for the book of Esther, and even its absence is probably an accident. However, there is not a single copy of any book from the New Testament to be found among them. There are, though, in the scrolls, a number of statements and ideas that would eventually evolve into portions of the Christian canon and that anticipated the religious developments that were to come very soon. This is especially evident when comparing the War Scroll, in which God and his angels are described as joining the "Sons of

Light" (the Essenes) in wiping out their enemies the "Sons of Darkness," with the Gospel of Paul that says, "But you, brethren, are not in darkness ... For you are all sons of light and sons of the day ... " (1 Thess. 5:4–5) and with the Letters of John that say " ... he who walks in the darkness does not know where he goes. While you have the light, believe in the light, that you may become sons of light" (John 12:35–36).

Both the Silver Amulet Scrolls and the Dead Sea Scrolls demonstrate the importance of discovering ancient texts. Most material artifacts found by biblical archaeologists are mute, without a voice, and must be interpreted by those who find them. Ancient texts and inscriptions, if able to be translated, literally speak volumes to both the archaeologists and the general public.

Chapter 10
From Herod the Great
to Jesus of Nazareth

Just as there are many questions remaining to be answered, from an archaeological point of view, regarding the account in the Hebrew Bible, so there are many remaining to be answered regarding the account in the Christian Bible. Of primary interest to New Testament biblical archaeologists and the general public are topics such as archaeological evidence for the historical Jesus; whether Herod's and Jesus' tombs have been discovered; if John the Baptist could have been an Essene; what it was like to live in cities such as Caesarea, Capernaum, and Sepphoris during this time; and what archaeology can tell us about the lives of the apostles.

Biblical archaeology of the New Testament generally is concerned with events that occurred immediately before, during, and after the life of Jesus, from the time of Herod in 40 BCE until the death of the apostles toward the end of the first century CE. The archaeology of the New Testament must cover the lands of Israel and Jordan (the Holy Land), as well as Turkey, Greece, and Italy in order to accommodate the voyages of Paul around the Mediterranean and the death of Peter in Rome. Overall, the archaeology of the Christian Bible covers a much shorter period of time (approximately two hundred years) and a much smaller geographical area (the Mediterranean region) than does archaeology of the Hebrew Bible (which covers about 1,500 years and most of the ancient Near East).

To begin with Herod the Great, we know that Herod's father, Antipater, was appointed commissioner of Judaea by Julius Caesar after the year 49 BCE. At the same time, Herod and his brother Phasael were appointed district commissioners. When their father died, Herod and his brother took over as commissioners of Judaea, but they soon faced a rebellion in the year 40 BCE. Herod's brother was captured and eventually killed, but Herod escaped across the desert to the fortress of Masada. There he left his family and his fiancée, Mariamne, along with eight hundred troops, and continued on to Rome to seek the assistance of Mark Antony and the Roman Senate. The Senate viewed his entreaties favorably, and it designated Herod as the "King of the Jews." Thus confirmed, Herod returned to Judaea, retrieved his family and fiancée, took over Jerusalem, and proceeded to rule Judaea for the next several decades.

Herod continued to fortify Masada over the course of his reign. Although he never had to take refuge at Masada, his building activities there marked the beginning of a reign filled with construction projects across the length and breadth of the land over which he ruled. Of these, one of the best known is the city and port he built at a coastal site south of modern-day Haifa.

Herod named the city Caesarea Maritimae ("Caesarea by the Sea") to honor his patron, the Roman emperor Caesar Augustus. The city was built on top of the remains of earlier construction and took approximately twelve years to build, from 22 to 10 BCE. In 6 CE, after Herod's death, Caesarea became the capital of the Roman province of Palestine. It retained that status for more than six hundred years, until 641 CE when Islamic armies overran the city. Even after that date, the city continued to play an important role, especially through the Crusader (1099–1271 CE) and Mamluke (1250–1517 CE) periods.

Excavations at the site have revealed an amphitheater, a theater (now restored, in which modern musical and theatrical events are held), a hippodrome, a palace, an aqueduct, and marketplaces, as well as warehouses and harbor facilities. These excavations have taken place nearly continuously for much of the past half-century by various Italian, American, and Israeli archaeological teams. That work continues to the present.

Thus far, the discovery at Caesarea of perhaps the greatest importance to biblical archaeology is an inscription in Latin dating to 30 CE that mentions Pontius Pilate, the prefect (or governor) of Palestine infamously connected with Jesus in the New Testament. The inscription was found in the theater at Caesarea during the Italian excavations in 1961. It records a dedication by Pontius Pilate to the Emperor Tiberius. Three of the fragmentary lines read: *Tiberieum/[Pon]tius Pilatus/[Praef]ectus Iuda[eae]*— which translates as "Tiberius/Pontius Pilate/Prefect of Judaea." The full inscription is believed to have read: "Pontius Pilate, the Prefect of Judaea, has dedicated to the people of Caesarea a temple in honor of Tiberius." This is the only inscription on stone known to mention Pontius Pilate and confirms the title given to him, previously known only from the New Testament.

Herod undertook a number of other building projects besides Masada and Caesarea. The one for which he is most famous was in Jerusalem—the renovation of the Temple Mount and the alterations to the Second Temple that stood upon it. On the same site had stood Solomon's Temple (the First Temple), which was destroyed by the Neo-Babylonians in 586 BCE. As described in the book of Ezra, Cyrus the Great of Persia authorized the rebuilding of the destroyed structure. Construction of the Second Temple began by 535 BCE and was completed about 516 BCE. With relatively little alteration, the Second Temple then stood on the same site for the next five centuries. In one sense, when Herod undertook his rebuilding project he was constructing what was really the third Hebrew temple on the site; however, because ritual sacrifices continued during the building process, it maintained continuity with the Second Temple and retained that name.

Herod's constructs enormously expanded the Temple Mount during the years 19–10 BCE, so that it covered an area the size of fifteen American football fields. It is still approximately the same size today. His renovations to the Second Temple made it the eighth wonder of the ancient world, and it is often referred to as Herod's Temple. According to Josephus, it appeared to travelers "like a mountain covered with snow."

Many of the events attributed to Jesus in the New Testament occurred in and around this Temple complex. Jesus even prophesized the destruction of the Temple (Matt. 21:12–14, 24:1–3)—a prophesy that came to pass at the hand of the Romans under Titus in 70 CE—but only a few traces of the Temple have been uncovered to date, probably because the destruction of this area by the Romans was so thorough.

One of the most exciting Herodian discoveries in recent years was made by Ehud Netzer of the Hebrew University in Jerusalem, at the site of Herodium, Herod's desert fortress located some seven miles south of Jerusalem. Netzer has been excavating at Herodium since 1972, as part of a long career in which he has uncovered remains of Herod's building program at many sites. Until recently, Netzer's excavations had focused on the lower palace built at the site. This is a huge palace, essentially the size of a small town, known as Lower Herodium. The excavators uncovered palatial buildings, gardens, warehouses, pools, and stables.

The most prominent feature at Herodium is a cone-shaped artificial mountain that Herod had constructed by adding fill to a much-smaller natural hill and raising it artificially until it was so high that it could be seen from Jerusalem. The top was fully 2,460 feet above sea level and was shaped so that it appeared to be a volcanic crater. Within this crater, Herod built a second, fortified palace consisting of a huge circular courtyard with buildings, a reception area, and a Roman bath, all surrounded by four guard towers.

The Roman historian Josephus says that Herod's body was brought to Herodium after he died at Jericho in 4 BCE. In a long and winding procession, Herod's sons and relatives marched next to the bier upon which Herod's body lay clothed in a purple robe, with a diadem and a crown of gold upon his head and a scepter lying beside his right hand. The bier was made of solid gold and studded with precious stones. As Josephus tells us, Herod's relatives "were followed by the guards, the Thracian contingent, Germans and Gauls, all equipped as for war. The reminder of the troops marched in front, armed and in orderly array, led by their commanders and subordinate officers; behind these came five hundred of Herod's servants and freedmen, carrying spices. The body was thus conveyed for a distance of two hundred furlongs to Herodium, where, in accordance with the directions of the deceased, it was interred. So ended Herod's reign."

Josephus does not describe the location of Herod's grave or mausoleum. After having searched for years without success in the area of the lower palace, Netzer refocused his attention in 2006 on an area midway up the artificial hill, between the upper and lower palaces. Almost immediately he and his staff found indications that they were finally looking in the proper place. They uncovered pieces of a monumental limestone sarcophagus and mausoleum, including various architectural elements such as decorated urns. Unfortunately, both the sarcophagus and the mausoleum were badly shattered, and they found only a portion of the ten-meter-square podium, built of large white ashlars (squared-off stones, a basic building block of masonry), on which the mausoleum would once have rested.

Netzer has suggested that the tomb was that of Herod the Great, based on the architectural fragments recovered as well as its general location, and believes that it was destroyed by Jewish zealots during the First Jewish Revolt against Rome from 66–70 CE when, according to Josephus, the rebels took over the site. Only a small number of human bones have been found at the site, and no identifying inscriptions have yet come to light, so while most scholars agree that Netzer has now solved one of the great New Testament mysteries—where was Herod's tomb?—complete confirmation is not yet available.

It was during the reign of King Herod, from 37 to 4 BCE, that Jesus was born—sometime between 7 and 4 BCE. According to the account in the New Testament, Herod attempted to dispose of this new "King of the Jews" by ordering the massacre of all male children in Bethlehem. But Jesus and his parents escaped to Egypt, where they remained until they received the news of Herod's death (Matt. 2:1–18).

Archaeology has not yet been able to shed any direct light on the birth, life, or death of Jesus. That is to say, there is not yet any archaeological evidence for the historical Jesus—or any of the apostles for that matter. Archaeology deals with the physical residue of the past, whether the remains of buildings, pottery fragments, or inscriptions on stone or papyrus. Therefore, unless one finds the actual remains of a body, the tools of archaeology can rarely provide evidence for the existence of a specific individual or group of individuals who lived in the distant past.

However, the failure of biblical archaeologists and pseudo-archaeologists to provide confirmatory evidence of the life of Jesus and the apostles has not been for lack of trying. The most recent attempt in this regard concerns the so-called Lost Tomb of Jesus, which was in the headlines in 2007 and 2008 as the result of a book and a documentary film with the same title. The documentary, by filmmakers Simcha Jacobovici and James Cameron, was featured on the Discovery Channel. The book was written by Jacobovici and Charles Pellegrino. In both the film and the book, Jacobovici claimed that the tomb of Jesus had been discovered in Jerusalem three decades earlier, in 1980.

In fact, the tomb—better known to archaeologists as the Talpiot Tomb—had indeed been accidentally discovered in 1980, during demolition work by construction workers laying the foundations for an apartment complex. Amos Kloner, district archaeologist for the Israel Department of Antiquities (now the Israel Antiquities Authority) in the area of Jerusalem, arranged for a quick salvage excavation of the tomb, directed by Yosef Gath. The final report of the excavations was published in 1996 by Kloner, now an associate professor of archaeology at Israel's Bar-Ilan University. There was no mention in the report of any possible connection of the tomb to Jesus or any members of his family, nor was there any reason that there should have been, for there was no link to be made.

Jacobovici's documentary was extensively criticized by archaeologists, who protested the manipulation of data and the leaps of faith involved in making such a claim. Jodi Magness, a biblical archaeologist and professor of religious studies at the University of North Carolina at Chapel Hill, said that the claim was sensationalistic and without any scientific basis or support. Joe Zias, a former curator of anthropology and archaeology at the Israel Antiquities Authority who was involved in the original excavation of the tomb, described the film as intellectually and scientifically dishonest. As far as professional archaeologists are concerned, the tomb of Jesus and his family remains undiscovered and, in fact, is more likely to have been located in their home town of Nazareth than in Jerusalem.

Apart from debunking the claims of irresponsible filmmakers, archaeologists can shed light on what the material culture was like at the time that Jesus and the apostles lived—for instance, what people ate, what they wore, and what their houses and buildings looked like in the cities of the Galilee, Sepphoris, Capernaum, and Jerusalem. In this way, archaeology can, to a certain extent, flesh out the details found in the writings of the apostles and of the historian Josephus. For instance, the excavators of the city of Sepphoris—located just four miles from Nazareth in the Galilee—describe life there during the first century CE as largely Jewish, rather than Hellenistic or Roman, as had previously been thought.

Sepphoris served as the capital of the Galilee first in 20 CE and then again from 61 CE. In the intervening four decades, the new city of Tiberias on the Sea of Galilee served as the capital. Sepphoris was no backwater. As Eric Meyers, a biblical archaeologist at Duke University and one of the excavators of Sepphoris, has said, it was architecturally sophisticated, "with paved and colonnaded streets; water installations, possibly including a bathhouse on the eastern plateau and some sort of public water works nearer the acropolis; multistory buildings; and major public structures, including a large columned building also on the eastern plateau."

Similarly, the excavators of Capernaum, the town by the Sea of Galilee where Jesus settled and preached in the years before he left for Jerusalem, have found not only specific buildings—such as the synagogue and churches built on top of the traditional location for the house of St. Peter—but have produced evidence that life in Capernaum was fairly prosperous in the first century CE. John Laughlin, a professor of religion at Averett University, notes that "far from being a poor, isolated village, Capernaum, the center of Jesus' Galilean ministry, was quite prosperous . . . In the centuries that followed, Capernaum expanded and continued to prosper, in part as a Christian pilgrim center. . . . " It seems that the tourist trade then, like now, provided the local economy with a boost, from which it has benefited ever since.

Chapter 11
From the Galilee Boat to the Megiddo Prison Mosaic

Archaeological discoveries relating to the Bible frequently come about in unexpected ways. For instance, in 1985 and 1986, the country of Israel was stricken with a severe drought. During the drought, the Sea of Galilee—otherwise known as Lake Tiberias—dropped dramatically, and great stretches of the lakebed became visible for the first time in hundreds of years. Near Capernaum, the receding waters of the Sea of Galilee left exposed an important artifact that lay waiting to be discovered.

Moshe and Yuval Lufan, two brothers from nearby Kibbutz Ginnosar, jumped at the chance to explore the newly revealed stretches of muddy land. As Shelley Wachsmann, a biblical and nautical archaeologist now at Texas A&M University, tells the story, a tractor that had become stuck in the mud of the lakebed churned up a few ancient coins while trying to break free of the muck. The two young men scoured the area and discovered a few ancient iron nails before spying a boat buried so deeply in the mud that only its outline was visible. Wachsmann, who at the time was an inspector of underwater antiquities for the Israel Antiquities Authority, was sent to investigate the find. A few days of digging in and around the boat uncovered a cooking pot and an oil lamp, both of which dated to the Roman period. Because the discovery of the boat had been leaked to the media and because the water level of the lake was once again rising, a more formal excavation had to begin without delay; that is to say, without the usual preplanning and fund-raising, which can take months and even years.

The entire excavation lasted only eleven days. In that span of time, working night and day, the archaeologists, conservators, and numerous volunteers from around the country managed to unearth what was left of the hull and superstructure of the boat. They encased all of the remains in a polyurethane "straitjacket," as Wachsmann calls it, and floated it over to the Yigal Allon Museum at Kibbutz Ginnosar. There, a pool was quickly built and the encased boat was lifted into it. After years of conservation work by Orna Cohen and her team at the museum, the boat went on display to the public, where it can be seen today in a special wing of the building.

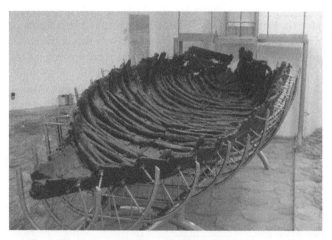

10. The Galilee Boat, on display in the Yigal Allon Museum at Kibbutz Ginnosar, was discovered in Lake Tiberias during a drought in 1986. Probably dating to a period from the late first century BCE to the late first century CE, it may shed light on the New Testament stories concerning Jesus' activities in and around the Sea of Galilee.

The excavators concluded that the boat was made primarily of cedar planking with an oak frame, although five other types of wood were also used in its construction. The boat was 26.5 feet long, 7.5 feet wide, and 4.5 feet high, with a rounded stern. It probably had a sternpost, which served to support a rudder and a mast, so that it could be sailed as well as rowed. It most likely had a crew of five, with two rowers per side plus a helmsman, and could perhaps have accommodated as many as ten passengers. Wachsmann hypothesizes that the boat, after possibly having a long and useful life, had ended up being used as scrap, with many of its still-usable timbers removed. The remaining part of the hull was pushed out into the lake, where it sank and then remained, until it was discovered nearly two thousand years later.

Seventeen datable pieces of pottery—including the intact lamp and cooking pot discovered during the first days—were found during the excavation. All point to a period from the late first century BCE to ca. 70 CE, that is, from a few decades before until a few decades after the lifetime of Jesus. Radiocarbon dating confirmed these results. The wood from the boat was dated to between 120 BCE and 40 CE. At the very latest, the boat sank some time around the First Jewish Revolt against Rome, which lasted from 66 to 70 CE. At the earliest, it may have gone down during Jesus' own lifetime.

The discovery of the boat—the only one known from this time period in the region—has already shed light on the sailing and boat-building practices of the day, since archaeologists are able to physically examine its features and the method of its construction, rather than simply hypothesizing about them based only on pictures from mosaics or written descriptions in the Bible. Unfortunately, it is not clear who owned the boat or whether it was ever actually related to any of the events depicted in the New Testament stories concerning Jesus' ministry in and around the Sea of Galilee.

Other objects associated with New Testament stories have been found by biblical archaeologists working in the Holy Land. Some are found during regularly scheduled excavations at sites like Sepphoris or Capernaum; others are initially found by accident, with the archaeologists quickly called in. In the latter category is the burial tomb and ossuary of Caiaphas, one of the most infamous figures associated with the life of Jesus. Caiaphas was high priest in Jerusalem in the years from 18 to 36 CE, which spans the time that Jesus was said to have been arrested and put on trial (John 18:12–14, 24–28; Luke 3:1–2). He is perhaps best known for saying of Jesus that it was better "to have one man die for the people than to have the whole nation destroyed" (John 11:49–53 [NRSV]; 18:14).

In 1990, the so-called Ossuary of Caiaphas—a stone box that may contain the bones of Caiaphas or members of his family—was discovered when a heavy dump truck broke through the roof of a burial cave during construction of a water park in Jerusalem's Peace Forest, located to the south of the Temple Mount and just below the Haas Tayelet (Promenade). Subsequently excavated by Zvi Greenhut of the Israel Antiquities Authority, the tomb is in a large cemetery, which has rock-cut burial chambers dating from the first century BCE through the first century CE.

There were a dozen ossuaries found in this one family tomb. All contained bones collected from bodies that had decomposed. The bones had been subsequently placed into these stone boxes as a secondary burial. This practice allowed the bodies of those who had died more recently to be laid out in the limited number of rock-cut niches in the tomb—there to decompose and eventually be moved into stone boxes of their own. One of the ossuaries had the word "Qafa" (Aramaic for the Greek name Caiaphas) scratched on the outside of the stone box. This was the first indication to archaeologists that they may have stumbled upon the tomb of the Caiaphas family.

Several of the ossuaries in the tomb contained the bones of more than one body. One ornately decorated limestone ossuary held the remains of six different individuals. Five of the bone sets contained within it were from an adult woman, a teenage boy, a young child, and two infants, but one set was from a man thought to have been about sixty years old when he died. It is this set of bones that has been tentatively identified as those of Caiaphas of the New Testament. An inscription incised two times on the outside of the stone box, "Yehosef bar Qafa" and "Yehosef bar Qayafa," can be translated as Aramaic variations on the Greek words "Joseph, son of Caiaphas" or perhaps even "Joseph, of the family Caiaphas."

The Roman historian Josephus says that Caiaphas' full name was Joseph Caiaphas, but that he was commonly referred to simply as Caiaphas—"Joseph, who was also called Caiaphas, of the high priesthood" (Josephus, *Antiquities of the Jews* 18.2.2, 18.4.3). Thus, the Joseph named in the ossuary inscription may be Caiaphas of the New Testament. However, this identification is by no means conclusive, for bodies could frequently be switched around in antiquity and even placed into ossuaries not originally meant for them.

Still, if this is the body of Caiaphas, he would be one of the few individuals described in the New Testament whose physical remains have been identified by archaeologists. Such individuals are surprisingly rare, so this discovery is more significant than it would be if the ossuary were uninscribed and the individual inside were unidentified. At the very least, if it is Caiaphas, the discovery would confirm that the people who play a role in the stories of the New Testament were real and not fictitious.

Even some of the most important people from the New Testament, such as John the Baptist, have left behind few traces of their existence. Thus, there was tremendous public interest when Shimon Gibson, a British archaeologist based in Jerusalem, announced that he had found a cave associated with John the Baptist. Gibson set out his evidence in a book titled *The Cave of*

John the Baptist: The Stunning Archaeological Discovery that has Redefined Christian History (2004).

Gibson had found pictures of a man with a staff, a dog, and a head incised onto the walls of a cave located near the village of Ain Kerem, the traditional birthplace of John the Baptist. He interpreted these as depictions of the story of the life of John the Baptist. In addition, he found an oval stone with a foot-shaped indentation, which he identified as having been used for ritual foot-washing. However, after spending five years excavating the cave, Gibson, and his colleague James Tabor, a Bible scholar from the University of North Carolina at Charlotte, admit that the cave drawings were not carved until at least the Byzantine period (fourth to seventh centuries CE) or later and that there is no direct link to John the Baptist. Gibson suggests that the cave may have been used by Christian monks or other religious advocates who believed that it was associated with John the Baptist, thus explaining the graphic depictions.

Although Gibson's interpretations are interesting, few scholars agree with them. In 2008, Joe Zias, formerly of the Israel Antiquities Authority, suggested instead that most of the images date to the Crusader period and that they are related not to John the Baptist but rather to Lazarus, the patron saint of leprosy. The treatment of leprosy included the washing of diseased feet.

Other interesting but unproven suggestions made in recent years concerning John the Baptist revolve around the emphasis that he placed on baptism and the fact that there are a large number of pools—probably Jewish ritual bathing pools used for purification (*miqva'ot*)—at the site of Qumran. The combination of the existence of these probable *miqva'ot* at Qumran, the idea that there may have been Essenes living at the site, and the suggestion that the idea of Christian baptism may have been derived from the Jewish practice of ritual immersion in *miqva'ot* has led a few scholars to suggest a three-part theory: that John may have lived at

Qumran at one point in his life; that he may have been an Essene (even though he is never identified as such either in the New Testament or by the historian Josephus); and that he may have gotten the idea of baptism from his use of the ritual pools at Qumran. Obviously there is much speculation involved in these suggestions, but little archaeology.

As for the actual ministry established by Jesus and his followers, some of the most interesting archaeological evidence was uncovered in November 2005 within a maximum-security prison located a few hundred yards away from the famous site of Megiddo (biblical Armageddon) in the Jezreel Valley. During construction work to expand the prison, workers uncovered an intriguing mosaic. It is in a building apparently used by Roman soldiers and currently thought to date to the third century CE.

The mosaic was placed into the floor in four separate sections, to the north, south, east, and west of what was probably once a table in the middle of the room that was used for the Eucharist. The eastern and western panels have only geometric patterns, but the northern and southern panels contain inlaid inscriptions in Greek. The northern panel records the name of the Roman soldier—Gaianus, a centurion—who paid for the mosaics, and the name Brutius, the craftsman who laid the mosaic. It features two fish, an early Christian image perhaps reflecting the miracle of loaves and fishes, which was used as a reference to Jesus for several centuries before the cross was adopted as a universal symbol for the religion. In translation, the inscription reads as follows: "Gaianus, also called Porphyrius, centurion, our brother, has made the pavement at his own expense as an act of liberality. Brutius carried out the work."

The southern panel contains two inscriptions. On the right (or eastern) side of the panel is an inscription with four women's names. It asks the viewer to remember "Primilla and Cyriaca and Dorothea, and moreover also Chreste." On the left (or western) side of the panel is the most interesting inscription. It says that the Eucharistic table in the middle of the room was paid for by a woman named Akeptous: "The God-loving Akeptous has offered the table to God Jesus Christ as a memorial." This is the earliest inscription ever found in Israel—and perhaps anywhere in the world—that mentions Jesus Christ.

The people named in the inscriptions have not been identified, but they probably belonged to a Christian community thriving among the soldiers of the Roman Sixth Legion, who were based in the area during those centuries. Scholars have debated whether the building in which the mosaic was found was a church. It was unlikely to have been the type of church structure with which we are now familiar, since Christian churches as we know them did not exist during the third century CE. They did not appear until the fourth century CE, after Emperor Constantine's Edict of Milan in 313 CE, which declared that Christianity was a tolerated religion and could be practiced without fear of punishment. It was at this later time that buildings such as the Church of the Holy Sepulcher in Jerusalem and the Church of the Nativity in Bethlehem were first built.

Some scholars argue that the building housing the mosaic may have been a so-called house church. These were apparently in use during the second and the third centuries CE, when Christianity was a forbidden religion; at that time, it was prudent to make places of Christian worship as inconspicuous as possible. In that era, places of worship were known by various names, including *ecclesi* and *domus Dei* (House of God).

At the time the mosaics were apparently laid, Christianity was considered to be an illegal religion in the Roman Empire, and its practitioners could be punished. However, the Roman authorities frequently turned a blind eye to the activities of adherents of a variety of outlawed religions—including the so-called mystery religions such as the worship of Eastern gods Mithras, Osiris, or

Orpheus—so long as the adherents of these religions revered the official Roman pantheon of gods and goddesses as well. Nevertheless, the province of Syria Palestine, as it was called at the time, including the region around Megiddo, was within the domain of the Roman Empire in the third century CE, and those named in the mosaic inscriptions may have been putting their lives in jeopardy by revealing their identity. That their names were so prominently inscribed perhaps speaks to the depth of their personal faith. On the other hand, if the dating of the building is off by a century, then it would have existed when it was allowable to practice Christianity without fear of punishment, and the story would not be quite as dramatic.

By this point, however, we are beyond the events depicted in the New Testament and have moved past the furthest boundaries of biblical archaeology and into the archaeology of the Byzantine and Late Antique period, which is another topic altogether.

Chapter 12
Fabulous finds or fantastic forgeries?

Some of the most interesting recent debates in biblical archaeology concern three objects that have come to the fore since the 1990s and the turn of the new millennium. These objects are either among the most important ever announced in the field of biblical archaeology or among the greatest hoaxes ever perpetrated upon a gullible public. They include an inscribed ivory pomegranate possibly from the Temple of Solomon in Jerusalem; the James Ossuary, which has an inscription proclaiming it to be the burial box of James, the brother of Jesus; and the Jehoash Tablet, upon which is written an inscription purportedly documenting repairs made to Solomon's Temple by King Jehoash, who ruled in Jerusalem from ca. 836 to 798 BCE.

All three objects have captured the public's imagination and have been featured in *Biblical Archaeology Review*, a popularizing magazine edited and published by Hershel Shanks—a lawyer who founded the Biblical Archaeology Society in Washington, DC, and who has been called the world's most influential amateur biblical archaeologist. While all three artifacts have been pronounced by various scholars as possible forgeries, based upon examination of the objects involving high-powered microscopes, petrographic analysis of the materials involved, and analysis of the inscriptions themselves, they are vigorously defended as genuine by Shanks and a few scholars.

The story begins in 1979, when André Lemaire, an esteemed epigrapher and professor at the Sorbonne in Paris, walked into the shop of an antiquities dealer in Jerusalem. He asked if the dealer had any objects with ancient Semitic inscriptions. This is not considered to be good practice by biblical archaeologists today, since it encourages a black market in antiquities, but standards and practices were different then. Lemaire was shown a small ivory pomegranate less than two inches tall, which was said to belong to an anonymous collector. The pomegranate was made from the canine tooth of a hippopotamus. Part of the main body was broken off, as were two of the six original petals rising from the stem. Running in a ring at the top of the body, just below where it meets the neck, were letters incised into the ivory. It was an inscription written in paleo-Hebrew, the letter-writing system that was used in Judah up until the return of those exiled to Babylon from 586 to 539 BCE.

After taking photographs and studying the inscription under a microscope, Lemaire went home to Paris. Eventually he published a scholarly article in *Revue Biblique* in 1981, followed by a popular article in *Biblical Archaeology Review* in 1984. He identified the pomegranate as part of a wand or scepter, the shaft of which would have been attached to a small hole that can still be seen in the base of the pomegranate. He dated it to the eighth century BCE and suggested that it probably belonged to the priests serving in the Temple in Jerusalem. Lemaire reached this startling conclusion based upon the partially broken inscription, which he reconstructed as reading *lby[t yhw]h qdsû khnm* ("Belonging to the Tem[ple of the Lor]d [Yahweh], holy to the priests"). If his analysis were correct, the pomegranate would be the first sacred object ever identified as coming from Solomon's Temple.

Shortly thereafter, the ivory pomegranate was illegally smuggled out of Israel and went on display at an exhibition in Paris in 1985. Three years later, after an additional private authentication by Nahman Avigad of the Hebrew University in Jerusalem, it was sold to the Israel Museum for $550,000. The huge price is generally agreed to be the result of the authentications of the pomegranate and its inscription by Lemaire and Avigad. To highlight its importance, the ivory pomegranate was put on exhibit sitting alone in splendid isolation within a glass case in an otherwise-empty room in the Israel Museum.

In 2004, however, the pomegranate was suddenly removed from display, and the museum issued a press release stating that the inscribed piece had been declared a forgery. In fact, a panel of experts, who first met in September 2004, had concluded that the pomegranate itself was authentic, but that the inscription was a recent addition. Their report stated: "In contrast to the antiquity of the pomegranate itself, the inscription and the patina-like material on the inscription and around it are a recent forgery.... The inscription was inscribed on the pomegranate after it had already been broken in ancient times, causing some new breaks to occur due to the pressure forced by the engraving tool on the edge of the old break and causing the incompletion of the [Hebrew letters] taw, he and yod in relation to the break in the pomegranate."

This was not the first time that the authenticity of the pomegranate and its inscription had been called into question, but now it seemed to fit a pattern that had emerged, in which a group of dealers and collectors allegedly conspired to add forged inscriptions to otherwise-authentic pieces in an effort to increase their value. The pomegranate has since been examined several times by additional experts who used microscopic examination designed to determine whether the inscription was carved before or after the large piece of the body broke off. Their reasoning was simple—if the inscription were authentic, the letters should continue straight into the ancient break without pause. If it were inscribed in recent times, the letters would probably end a few millimeters before the break, because the forger would have been afraid of breaking off more of the original ivory if he continued his cuts. In the end, all the experts agreed that the pomegranate itself is an authentic relic, probably originally dating to the Late Bronze Age, that is, to the thirteenth or twelfth centuries BCE. However, they could not definitively answer the question of whether the inscription carved upon it dates to the eighth century BCE, i.e., the time of Solomon's Temple, or to the late twentieth century CE. The question remains unanswered despite all the scientific testing. Everything rests upon three small Hebrew letters.

Better known to the general public than the ivory pomegranate is the so-called James Ossuary, which was announced with great fanfare at a press conference held in October 2002 by Shanks on behalf of the *Biblical Archaeology Review*, which broke the story and ran it as the cover story for the November/December 2002 issue. Ossuaries are fairly common discoveries in the Holy Land; they are stone boxes that contained bones from a body (or bodies) that had decomposed and subsequently been collected and placed into the box as a secondary burial (see chap. 11). What makes this ossuary unusual is the inscription carved into one of the sides in Aramaic: *Yaakov bar Yoseph, Achui de Yeshua* ("James, son of Joseph, brother of Jesus").

When the world media reported the existence of the James Ossuary the morning after the press conference, excitement ran high. It was hailed as a major discovery—the first possible physical evidence for the existence of Jesus ever to be found. Nightly TV newscasts led with the story, which was also carried by most of the major newspapers and magazines in the United States and around the world.

The James Ossuary was owned by Oded Golan, a Tel Aviv antiquities collector who says that he purchased it in the mid-1970s and that it was stored on the balcony of his parents' apartment for a number of years until he moved it to his own apartment. Golan's interest in antiquity began while he was still quite young: a ten-year-old Golan is said to have discovered a now-famous small cuneiform tablet while walking around the site of Hazor as a tourist.

Golan claims that he had seen and known of the inscription on the ossuary since he first purchased it from an East Jerusalem antiquities dealer in the Old City of Jerusalem, but that he did not initially realize its significance. He says he thought "that the inscription referred to three generations because the only thing that [he] could read with certainty was the three names, Yaakov, Yosef and Yeshua." He also said that he did not know that Jesus had any siblings.

According to Golan, in 2002 he invited André Lemaire, the Semitic epigrapher at the Sorbonne, to look at another one of the forty ossuaries in his collection, in order to decipher a four-line inscription in Aramaic. While doing so, Lemaire asked Golan if he owned any other inscribed objects. Golan showed Lemaire various photographs, including a picture of the James Ossuary that was in storage at that time. At Lemaire's request, Golan retrieved the ossuary and allowed Lemaire to study it and its inscription firsthand during a subsequent visit. Lemaire then prepared an article for publication in Hershel Shanks' *Biblical Archaeology Review*, which was in itself a bit strange, since the initial publication should have been in a scholarly peer-reviewed journal rather than a popular magazine.

Before he published the article, Shanks asked Ada Yardeni, a leading Israeli epigrapher, to examine the authenticity of the inscription. In addition, he asked members of the Geological Survey of Israel (GSI) to examine and confirm the authenticity of the ossuary itself. Having received a confirmation of authenticity from all parties, Shanks scheduled the international press conference for October 2002, to be held in conjunction with the publication of the ossuary as the cover story in the November/ December issue of *Biblical Archaeology Review*, as mentioned earlier. The entire event was recorded for a future broadcast on the Discovery Channel by Simcha Jacobovici, the same Toronto filmmaker who would later be responsible for the Lost Tomb of Jesus fiasco.

An exhibition of the ossuary was hastily arranged for the following month, November 2002, at the Royal Ontario Museum (ROM) in Toronto. Such speed is virtually unheard of in the museum world, where exhibits usually take years of planning before coming to fruition. But, the annual meetings of the Society of Biblical Literature, the American Academy of Religion, and the American Schools of Oriental Research were all scheduled to be held in Toronto in mid-November, and these would bring thousands of biblical experts and archaeologists to the city, which explains the interest of the Royal Ontario Museum.

The exhibit went off as planned, drawing a reported 100,000 visitors in the short time that the ossuary was on display. The only hitch was that the ossuary had been shipped from Israel to Canada in substandard packing—literally in a cardboard box and bubble-wrap—and had arrived in Toronto badly damaged, with large cracks in several places, including one that ran right through the inscription. The conservators at the ROM worked to restore the ossuary in time for the exhibition. This presented an opportunity for the staff to do some more testing of the ossuary and led to additional data and questions concerning the authenticity of the inscription.

After the exhibition, the ossuary was returned to Oded Golan in Israel, much to the relief of the Israel Antiquities Authority (IAA), which had granted an export permit to Golan without realizing the potential importance of the ossuary. Golan eventually handed over the ossuary to the IAA for testing by a panel of fourteen researchers.

In the meantime, Shanks was busy writing a book about the ossuary, which he co-authored with Ben Witherington III, a professor of New Testament at Asbury Theological Seminary in Lexington, Kentucky. The book appeared in March 2003, with a foreword by Lemaire. That same month, the panel of experts commissioned by the IAA met for the first time and was given its marching orders—to determine the authenticity of the James Ossuary and its inscription. The fourteen experts were split into two committees. One group of eight scholars was designated as the Writing and Content Committee and instructed to look at the inscription on the ossuary. The other group of six scholars was designated as the Materials and Patina Committee and instructed to look specifically at the material and composition of the ossuary.

The experts announced their findings in a report issued after a final joint meeting in mid-June 2003. Portions of the report were published the following year in the *Journal of Archaeological Science*. They concluded that while the ossuary was authentic, the inscription on it was not. As Orna Cohen, an experienced archaeological restorer and one of the panel experts, stated, the inscription "cuts through the original patina and is coated with a granular patina that appears to have been produced from chalk dust mixed with water and spread on the inscription." Another panel expert, Yuval Goren of Tel Aviv University, explained further: "The inscription was inscribed or cleaned in the modern period. Its coating is not a result of nature, and was probably accomplished by crumbling and dissolving chalk (or perhaps the powder falling from the engraving process) in hot water and spilling the suspension on the inscription and surrounding area in order to blur the freshly carved inscription."

The conclusion was not surprising to many in the world of biblical archaeology. However, there were discussions and disagreements, particularly on websites and interactive forums on the Internet, as to how much of the inscription had been forged. Some suggested that only the final portion "brother of Jesus" had been added by a forger. By that point, only a few people were still actively arguing that both the ossuary and its entire inscription were authentic. Those few who supported the claim of authenticity—principally Shanks, Witherington, and members of the original team who had first authenticated the ossuary and its inscription for its initial publication—contested the committee's conclusions, arguing that the panel members were biased and the tests and conclusions flawed. A few weeks later, in July 2003, authorities came to Golan's apartment to seize the ossuary. They found it stored on the seat of a toilet in a bathroom on the roof of his apartment building.

While the debate over the James Ossuary was still ongoing, rumors began to circulate about yet another object on the antiquities market—a black stone tablet with an inscription purportedly concerning King Jehoash's repairs to the First Temple during the ninth century BCE. Jehoash is known from the Hebrew Bible as a king who ruled over Judah from ca. 836 to 798 BCE. His repairs to the Temple are recounted in the Bible (2 Kings 12:1–21), which means that the stone tablet, if genuine, would immediately validate the historicity of the biblical account. It would also make this tablet the third object with potential links to biblical archaeology to appear on the market in recent decades.

When the world media first announced the existence of the Jehoash Tablet in 2003, excitement once again ran high, and again there were mentions on nightly TV newscasts and in most of the major newspapers and magazines. Professor Gabriel Barkay, discoverer of the tiny Silver Amulet Scrolls in Jerusalem, announced that if the tablet were genuine, it would be the most significant archaeological finding ever made in the Land of Israel.

Now that most of the available information has been published, it turns out that the existence of the Jehoash Tablet had been known to a select few for two years before the first rumors began to circulate in early 2003. However, it was not until *Biblical Archaeology Review* picked up the story in March of that year and featured the Jehoash Tablet on its cover in May that the story gained momentum, even as the initial hubbub about the James Ossuary finally began to die down.

As the story has been reported, the tablet was first shown to Joseph Naveh of the Hebrew University of Jerusalem during the summer of 2001. Naveh is considered to be one of the leading paleographers in Israel, an expert in the study of ancient writing. He received an anonymous phone call and then a photograph of the tablet before he agreed to examine the inscription itself. The meeting took place at a Jerusalem hotel. Naveh was shown the tablet by two men and was told that it had been found in the Kidron Valley east of the Temple Mount. Later reports said that the tablet had been originally uncovered in 1999 during illegal excavations on the Temple Mount by the Islamic Waqf, when the Marwani mosque was being built in the southeastern corner of the Mount, and that it had been dumped in the Kidron Valley along with all of the other dirt and artifacts that had been unearthed.

The tablet, made of black stone three inches thick and measuring almost a foot in length and nine inches in width, contains fifteen lines of text written in paleo-Hebrew letters, the script used before the Babylonian Exile. The inscription reads:

> [I am Yeho'ash son of A]haziah k[ing of . . . Ju]dah and I did
> [the work] just as the will[ing]ness of the heart of each man in the
> land and in the desert and in all the cities of Judah was complete to
> give the silver of the holy things amply, to acquire hewn stone and
> cypresses and copper of Edom, to do the work in faithfulness. And
> I performed the repair of the House and the walls round about and
> the ledge and the lattices and the staircases and the recesses and the
> doors. And may this day become an observance that the work may be
> successful. May Yahweh ordain his people with a blessing.

The first line, which would have contained the name Jehoash, is broken off and is therefore almost totally reconstructed by the scholars, based upon the name Ahaziah, his father.

The tablet was next brought for analysis and authentication to the Geological Survey of Israel (GSI), where it was discovered that carbon particles and minute globules of pure gold were embedded within the patina on the face of the tablet and in the incised letters. Did the carbon pieces and gold globules come from burnt wood and melted gold when the Temple was destroyed by fire in 586 BC? The geologists who examined the tablet were convinced of this scenario.

They published their preliminary analysis and conclusions in 2003, in the journal *Geological Survey of Israel Current Research*, concluding that "An event took place, in which pure gold was heated to a temperature of more than 1000 °C and melted, so that gold globules were formed." They stated that "A thin brown patina developed. . . . Gold globules and carbon fragments were entrapped within the patina" and that "There is no evidence that the patina was artificially added to the stone." They then went beyond the standard analysis and authentication process and, quite unusually, included a "Hypothetical Scenario" in their GSI publication, suggesting

> The tablet could have been originally emplaced in Jerusalem about 2800 years B.P. (Before Present) and remained there for about 200 years. . . . Then, when the Babylonians destroyed Jerusalem about 2600 B.P. (586 B.C.E.), the tablet was broken and was subsequently buried in the rubble. Upon burial, the patina started to develop on the tablet. . . . The source of gold may have been gold artifacts or gold-gilded items that existed in Jerusalem at that time. As Jerusalem was set on fire (Kings II 25, 9), some of this gold could have melted in the conflagration, injected to the air and re-solidified there, to settle later as minute globules on the ground. These were

x

Biblical Archaeology

later incorporated within the patina that developed on the buried tablet.

In the meantime, however, the tablet was reanalyzed by the same committee of experts that had been set up by the Israel Antiquities Authority to examine the James Ossuary. As with the James Ossuary, they were asked to determine the authenticity of the Jehoash Tablet. The committees' findings concerning the tablet were contained in the same report as those concerning the ossuary, issued after the final joint meeting in mid-June 2003. Again portions were published the following year, this time in the journal *Tel Aviv*.

Goren and his colleagues on the Materials and Patina Committee said specifically that the micromorphologic, petrographic, and oxygen isotopic composition of the patina covering the letters and the surface of the inscription clearly indicate that it was artificially created in recent times and that the tablet is therefore a modern forgery. They were led to this conclusion in part by noticing that there were two different types of patina on the surface of the tablet. One type was strongly attached to the surface, but was found only on the uninscribed reverse side of the tablet. The other was "an artificial mixture of elements" including calcite, clay, charcoal, and gold.

Goren and his co-authors said that this second type of patina, which covered the letters of the inscription, "could not have been formed under the natural conditions that have prevailed in the Judean Hills over the last 3500 years" and was most likely a "fake patina." This, in turn, suggests that it was "artificially prepared . . . with hot water, and deposited onto the surface (and inscription) of the tablet. Heated water was used to harden and ensure good adhesion of the patina."

Moreover, they found that the tablet was not made of arkosic sandstone, originating in southern Israel or Jordan, as the original

Geological Survey of Israel geologists had concluded, but rather was made of metamorphic greywacke, which is not naturally found in Israel but is in Cyprus and areas farther west. Goren noted that such stones are sometimes found in Israel, where they were used in the construction of Crusader castles, having originally served as ballast on board ships coming from Cyprus. There is one such castle at Apollonia, not far from Tel Aviv. In any event, the Materials and Patina Committee reached the conclusion that the Jehoash Tablet is a modern forgery.

The Writing and Content Committee reached a similar conclusion regarding the inscription on the tablet. One member, Shmuel Ahituv of Ben Gurion University, concluded that the inscription was written by a speaker of modern Hebrew who composed a text that seemed biblical to him or her, but which was not grammatically correct. Another member, Avigdor Horowitz of Ben Gurion University, stated that the inscription attests to a lack of understanding of ninth century BCE Hebrew and that all of the various grammatical elements together "clearly prove that the text is a forgery."

Indeed, this meshed well with the conclusion that Naveh had already reached the first time that he saw the tablet, back in 2001. Even in that first meeting, Naveh was convinced that he was looking at a forgery, mainly because of problems with the inscription. Many other paleographers and epigraphers have since agreed, including Frank Cross of Harvard University and P. Kyle McCarter of Johns Hopkins University, who have documented rudimentary misspellings and grammatical mistakes in the inscription, which should not be present if it were authentically ancient. Cross concluded that there is "little doubt that we are dealing with a forgery . . . fortunately, it is a rather poor forgery." Christopher Rollston, of the Emmanuel School of Religion, acquiesced; he wrote, "The script of the Jehoash Inscription deviates so substantially from all provenanced Iron Age Hebrew inscriptions that it cannot, in my opinion, be seriously considered ancient."

In the interim, it became clear that Oded Golan was involved with the Jehoash Tablet, just as he was previously linked to the James Ossuary. The two individuals who originally showed the tablet to Joseph Naveh were apparently hired representatives who knew nothing about the tablet and had simply been paid to bring the tablet to the meeting set up in the Jerusalem hotel. Eventually, after some good detective work on the part of the IAA's Theft Prevention Unit, the truth of the situation emerged.

The tablet was in the possession of Golan, although he claimed that he was simply a middleman in the deal. He said that the tablet was actually owned by a now-deceased antiquities dealer named Abu-Yasser Awada, who had come into possession of the tablet and had asked Golan to help him sell it. Golan had agreed and had apparently enlisted a large and established law firm to work on his behalf, while he remained anonymously in the background. Rumor even had it that the tablet was offered to the Israel Museum for more than four million dollars. However, the museum's director says that the tablet was brought to the museum only for authentication in 2001 or 2002, before the investigations by the IAA had begun, and that no price was ever discussed.

Although their numbers are few, there are still those who argue for the authenticity—or possible authenticity—of the Jehoash Tablet and its inscription. Their arguments can be found primarily in the pages of the *Biblical Archaeology Review*. Although the GSI issued an official statement in June 2003, agreeing with the conclusions of the IAA committee, the original GSI geologists continue to maintain that their conclusions and hypothetical scenario regarding the tablet are correct. They presented their position again at the annual meeting of the Geological Society of America in 2005 and published an article in the *Journal of Archaeological Science* in 2008.

In March 2008, however, the American television news magazine *60 Minutes* broadcast an undercover video interview with an Egyptian craftsman in Cairo named Marco Samah Shoukri Ghatas (identified as Marko Sammech by *60 Minutes*), who stated that he did work for Golan over a period of fifteen years. When shown a photograph of the Jehoash Tablet, Ghatas said—on camera—that he had "inscribed several stone slabs that were just like this for [Oded] Golan . . . Golan brought me the text and I carved it onto the tablet."

According to a follow-up story in *Ha'aretz* in April 2008, Ghatas confessed—both to Egyptian authorities and to Amir Ganor, head of the IAA's Theft Prevention Unit—that he had "personally forged the Jehoash inscription, on the basis of the sketches brought to him by Oded Golan" and had manufactured numerous other items "according to specifications received from Golan." According to Ganor's testimony, Ghatas also admitted to "rinsing and smearing" the James Ossuary, apparently with an artificial patina.

When the police raided Golan's apartment, office, and a rented storage compartment in July 2003, they seized both the James Ossuary and the Jehoash Tablet. They also found soil in labeled bags from numerous excavation sites, tools and engraving equipment, half-finished royal seals, other inscriptions in various stages of production, epigraphic handbooks, a blank stone similar in size to the Jehoash Tablet, and other objects. In addition, they found photographs of a quartz bowl with an inscription in Egyptian hieroglyphs recording the fact that the commander of Egyptian Pharaoh Shishak's army had conquered the ancient city of Megiddo. The bowl had apparently been destroyed by Golan, but he had kept the photographs.

One thing that all three of the original objects—the pomegranate, ossuary, and tablet—had in common, apart from the fact that they may all be forgeries, is that they first surfaced on the art market and were of unknown provenance; that is, they had not been found in proper archaeological excavations. Had they been discovered during the course of controlled excavations by professional archaeologists, as were the Tel Dan Stele, the Tel Miqne/Ekron Inscription, and the Silver Amulet scrolls, they would have immediately assumed a place among the most important biblical artifacts ever found. As it is, the three objects serve as reminders for why most professional biblical archaeologists and professional journals refuse to publish or discuss objects from the art market that do not have a proper provenance or documented context.

Epilogue

Having overcome the sabotaging nihilism of the 1990s and the early part of the new millennium, and notwithstanding the ongoing debates regarding David and Solomon as well as the question of possible forgeries, biblical archaeology continues to benefit from new discoveries, especially ancient writing.

For instance, Aren Maeir of Bar Ilan University, digging at the Philistine city of Tel Safi/Gath in a level dating to the tenth or ninth century BCE, found a pottery sherd that may have the ancient equivalent of the name "Goliath" scratched on it. Although the sherd (and the name) almost certainly did not belong to David's Goliath, it does show that there was such a personal name used in the region at approximately the correct chronological period.

At the site of Tel Zayit, Ron Tappy of the Pittsburgh Theological Seminary found the oldest known written example of an abecedary (alphabet) yet discovered in the Holy Land. It was found incised (scratched) onto a thirty-eight-pound limestone boulder, which had been used as part of a stone wall. Dating to the late tenth century BCE, the abecedary at Tel Zayit is an important ancestor in the history of writing; the excavators suggest that "all successive alphabets in the ancient world (including non-Semitic ones, such as Greek) derived from the alphabet seen in the Tel Zayit Inscription."

And at the site of Khirbet Qeiyafa (possibly ancient Sha'arayim), Yossi Garfinkel of the Hebrew University of Jerusalem discovered a pottery sherd probably dating to the tenth century BCE with five inked lines of Hebrew, written using proto-Canaanite script, a precursor of the Hebrew alphabet. The words "king," "judge," and "slave" could be made out immediately, but the rest of the inscription was so faded that nothing more could be read by the naked eye. The ostracon was subsequently flown to the United States, where Greg Bearman, formerly of NASA's Jet Propulsion Laboratory at the California Institute of Technology, who has served as a pioneer in applying modern imaging technology to archaeology, used a variety of high-technology systems in Massachusetts and California to take further images, including two different imaging spectrometers (one that acquires the entire reflectance spectrum of a line at once and the other that creates both reflectance and fluorescence spectral images) and twelve-band spectral imaging with higher spatial resolution than the previous two methods. When all of the images have been analyzed, it should be possible to read the entire inscription; if so, the above advanced methods may be used on some of the fragmentary Dead Sea Scrolls and other ancient inscriptions.

As for nonwritten discoveries, biblical archaeologists Tom Levy of the University of California at San Diego and Mohammad Najjar of Jordan's Friends of Archaeology have published evidence that the site of Khirbat en-Nahas in Jordan, an ancient copper-production site, contains industrial smelting debris more than twenty feet deep. According to Levy, the radiocarbon dates may date the site, located in the biblical kingdom of Edom, to the tenth or ninth centuries BCE, some three hundred years earlier than previously thought—and could be related to the famous copper mines of King Solomon.

And as for Jerusalem, researchers have announced several major finds, including a layer of untouched and unexcavated remains dating to the time of the First Temple on top of Jerusalem's Temple Mount, found during repair work that was being conducted by the Islamic Waqf (which oversees the Mount). The deposit, which probably dates to the eighth through the sixth centuries BCE, contains pottery, bones, and other ancient remains, which are the first from this time period to be found on the Temple Mount. In addition, a wall, which probably dates to the first century BCE and which may be from the Second Temple, was found during the same repair work on top of Jerusalem's Temple Mount. It may be from one of the courts of the Temple; if so, it would help us begin to understand the layout of the Temple. At the same time, a quarry was found in Jerusalem that may have supplied massive stone blocks for the Second Temple. This is the first indication that such materials may have been procured locally. Finally, a huge city drain was found in Jerusalem, dating from the time of the First Jewish Revolt in the first century CE. It fits the description given by Josephus, the Jewish general turned Roman historian, of an escape route used during the Roman siege that destroyed the city and the Temple.

Clearly, there remains much to be discovered, and much to be excited about, in the field of biblical archaeology. Although the discipline is not a new field, having been seriously practiced for more than one hundred years, it has kept pace with modern developments. At its inception the principal tools were the pick and shovel. Now biblical archaeologists use magnetometers, ground-penetrating radar, electric resistivity meters, and satellite photography alongside traditional methods of excavation, enabling them to peer beneath the ground surface before physical excavation begins. Radiocarbon dating is used alongside time-honored chronological methods such as pottery seriation and typology. And biblical archaeologists are working hand in hand with specialists in ceramic petrography, residue analysis, and DNA analysis, in order to answer more anthropologically oriented questions concerning ethnicity, gender, trade, and the rise of rulership and complex societies.

Sometimes these tools help to confirm the biblical text and sometimes they do not. Upon occasion, the archaeologists can bring to life the people, places, and events discussed in the Bible. But biblical archaeology is not about proving or disproving the Bible; its practitioners are concerned with investigating the material culture of the lands and eras in question and reconstructing the culture and history of the Holy Land for a period lasting more than two thousand years. And that in itself is absolutely fascinating, for professionals and the general public alike.

References

Many of the details regarding the individuals, sites, and discoveries, including the translation of the Gezer Calendar, are derived from various entries in *The Oxford Encyclopedia of Archaeology in the Near East, vols. 1-5*, edited by Eric M. Meyers (New York: Oxford University Press, 1997). In addition, the Scripture quotations contained herein are from either the New Revised Standard Version Bible, copyright 1989 by the Division of Christian Education of the National Council of Churches of Christ in the U.S.A., or the New American Standard Bible®, copyright 1995 by The Lockman Foundation, and are used by permission. Some of the material herein originally appeared in different form in *From Eden to Exile: Unraveling Mysteries of the Bible* (Washington, DC: National Geographic Books, 2007) and "Raiders of the Faux Ark," *Boston Globe*, September 30, 2007, D1-2, both by the present author, and is used here by permission.

Part I

Chapter 1

Philip J. King, "Edward Robinson: Biblical Scholar," *Biblical Archaeologist* 46/4 (1983): 230-32.

Douglas L. Esse and Timothy P. Harrison, "Chapter One: History of Excavations," in *Megiddo 3: Final Report on the Stratum VI Excavations*, ed. Timothy P. Harrison (Chicago: University of Chicago Press, 2004), 1.

Amihai Mazar, *Archaeology of the Land of the Bible: 10,000–586 BCE* (New York: Doubleday, 1992), 10-21.

Neil A. Silberman, *Digging for God and Country: Exploration,*
Archaeology, and the Secret Struggle for the Holy Land, 1799–1917
(New York: Random House, 1982), 86, 99, 115, 123.

Siegfried H. Horn, "Why the Moabite Stone Was Blown to Pieces,"
Biblical Archaeology Review 12/3 (1986): 50–61.

J. Maxwell Miller and John H. Hayes, *A History of Ancient Israel and*
Judah, 2nd ed. (Louisville, KY: Westminster John Knox Press,
2006), 296 (Text 4).

André Lemaire, "'House of David' Restored in Moabite Inscription,"
Biblical Archaeology Review 20/3 (1994): 30–37.

Israel Finkelstein and Neil A. Silberman, *The Bible Unearthed:*
Archaeology's New Vision of Ancient Israel and the Origin of Its
Sacred Texts (New York: Free Press, 2001), 256–57.

George Adam Smith, preface to *The Historical Geography of the Holy*
Land (London: Hodder and Stoughton, 1894).

Chapter 2

J. Maxwell Miller and John H. Hayes, *A History of Ancient Israel and*
Judah, 2nd ed. (Louisville, KY: Westminster John Knox Press,
2006), 39–41.

Amihai Mazar, *Archaeology of the Land of the Bible: 10,000–586 BCE*
(London: Doubleday, 1992), 30, table 2.

Jonathan Tubb, "Most of What We Know about Gezer comes from
Macalister" (paper presented at the annual meetings of the
American Schools of Oriental Research, Boston, MA, November
19–22, 2008).

Thomas W. Davis, *Shifting Sands: The Rise and Fall of Biblical*
Archaeology (Oxford: Oxford University Press, 2004), 42–44.

Palestine Exploration Fund, "The Re-publication of *The Wilderness of*
Zin: (PEF Annual III) by C. L. Woolley and T. E. Lawrence."
Palestine Exploration Fund website, www.pef.org.uk/annuals/the-
re-publication-of-the-wilderness-of-zin-pef-annual-iii-by-cl-
woolley-and-te-lawrence.

Chapter 3

Peter D. Feinman, *William Foxwell Albright and the Origins of Biblical*
Archaeology (Berrien Springs, MI: Andrews University Press,
2004), passim.

Thomas W. Davis, *Shifting Sands: The Rise and Fall of Biblical Archaeology* (Oxford: Oxford University Press, 2004), 89–92.

P. L. O. Guy, *New Light from Armageddon* (Chicago: University of Chicago Press, 1931), 37–48.

Robert S. Lamon and Geoffrey M. Shipton, *Megiddo I: Season of 1925–1934 Strata I–V* (Chicago: University of Chicago Press, 1939), 32–47, 59.

Chapter 4

Bryant G. Wood, "Did the Israelites Conquer Jericho? A New Look at the Archaeological Evidence," *Biblical Archaeology Review* 16/2 (1990): 44–58.

Piotr Bienkowski, "Jericho Was Destroyed in the Middle Bronze Age, Not the Late Bronze Age," *Biblical Archaeology Review* 16/5 (1990): 45–46.

Bryant G. Wood, "Dating Jericho's Destruction: Bienkowski Is Wrong on All Counts," *Biblical Archaeology Review* 16/5 (1990): 47–49, 68–69.

Felicity Cobbing, "John Garstang's excavations at Jericho: A Cautionary Tale" (paper presented at the annual meetings of the American Schools of Oriental Research, Boston, MA, November 19–22, 2008).

Neil A. Silberman, *A Prophet from Amongst You: The Life of Yigael Yadin—Soldier, Scholar, and Mythmaker of Modern Israel* (New York: Addison Wesley Publishing Company, 1993), passim.

Josephus, *The Jewish War* 7.8–9, in *The New Complete Works of Josephus*, trans. William Whiston (Grand Rapids, MI: Kregel Publications, 1999), 925–34.

Yigael Yadin, *Masada: Herod's Last Fortress and the Zealot's Last Stand* (New York: Welcome Rain, 1998), passim.

Nachman Ben-Yehuda, *The Masada Myth: Collective Memory and Mythmaking in Israel* (Madison: University of Wisconsin Press, 1995), passim.

Chapter 5

Roni Reich, "The Israel Antiquities Authority," in *Biblical Archaeology Today, 1990. Proceedings of the Second International Congress on Biblical Archaeology; Jerusalem, June–July 1990*, ed. Avraham

Biran and Joseph Aviran (Jerusalem: The Israel Exploration Society, 1993), 27–30.

Israel Finkelstein and Neil A. Silberman, *The Bible Unearthed: Archaeology's New Vision of Ancient Israel and the Origin of Its Sacred Texts* (New York: Free Press, 2001), 243–45.

Jane M. Cahill, Karl Reinhard, David Tarler, and Peter Warnock. "It Had to Happen: Scientists Examine Remains of Ancient Bathroom." *Biblical Archaeology Review* 17/3 (1991): 64–69.

Jeffrey Blakely, "Conversations with Larry Toombs on the American Method" (paper presented at the annual meetings of the American Schools of Oriental Research, Boston, MA, November 19–22, 2008).

William G. Dever, *Archaeology and Biblical Studies: Retrospects and Prospects. The Winslow Lectures at Seabury-Western Theological Seminary, 1972* (Evanston, IL: Seabury-Western, 1974), 33.

William G. Dever, "Syro-Palestinian and Biblical Archaeology," in *The Hebrew Bible and Its Modern Interpreters*, ed. Douglas A. Knight and Gene M. Tucker (Philadelphia: Fortress Press, 1985), 31–74.

David Ilan, "Archaeology Adding to the Powder Keg," *Biblical Archaeology Review* 34/6 (2008): 36, 86.

Chapter 6

William M. Schniedewind, "Tel Dan Stela: New Light on Aramaic and Jehu's Revolt," *Bulletin of the American Schools of Oriental Research* 302 (1996): 77–78.

Hershel Shanks, "Face to Face: Biblical Minimalists Meet Their Challengers," *Biblical Archaeology Review* 23/4 (1997): 26–42, 66.

Philip R. Davies, "'House of David' Built on Sand," *Biblical Archaeology Review* 20/4 (1994): 54–55.

Aaron Demsky, "The Name of the Goddess of Ekron: A New Reading," *Journal of the Ancient Near Eastern Society* 25 (1997): 1–5.

Seymour Gitin, "Royal Philistine Temple Inscription Found at Ekron," *Biblical Archaeologist* 59/3 (1996): 181–82.

Seymour Gitin, Trude Dothan, and Joseph Naveh, "A Royal Dedicatory Inscription from Ekron," *Israel Exploration Journal* 48 (1997): 1–18.

J. Maxwell Miller and John H. Hayes, *A History of Ancient Israel and Judah*, 2nd ed. (Louisville, KY: Westminster John Knox Press, 2006), 418–19 (Text 12).

Seymour Gitin, "Excavating Ekron: Major Philistine City Survived by Absorbing Other Cultures," *Biblical Archaeology Review* 31/6 (2005): 40–56.

Eilat Mazar, "Excavate King David's Palace!" *Biblical Archaeology Review* 23/1 (1997): 50–57, 74.

———, "Did I Find King David's Palace?," *Biblical Archaeology Review* 32/1 (2006): 16–27, 70.

Israel Finkelstein, Ze'ev Herzog, Lily Singer-Avitz, and David Ussishkin, "Has King David's Palace In Jerusalem Been Found?" *Tel Aviv* 34 (2007): 142–64.

Israel Finkelstein and Neil A. Silberman, *The Bible Unearthed: Archaeology's New Vision of Ancient Israel and the Origin of Its Sacred Texts* (New York: Free Press, 2001), 342–44 and passim.

Israel Finkelstein, Amihai Mazar, and Brian B. Schmidt, *The Quest for the Historical Israel: Debating Archaeology and the History of Early Israel* (Atlanta, GA: Society of Biblical Literature, 2007).

Israel Finkelstein and Eliazer Piasetzky, "The Iron I-IIA in the Highlands and Beyond: 14C Anchors, Pottery Phases and The Shoshenq I Campaign," *Levant* 38 (2006): 45–61.

Etgar Lefkovits, "'Land of Milk and Honey' it is," *Jerusalem Post*, September 3, 2007.

Editor, "Digs Go Digital," *Biblical Archaeology Review* 35/1 (2009): 28–36.

Part II

Chapter 7

Eric H. Cline, "Raiders of the Faux Ark," *Boston Globe*, September 30, 2007, D1–2.

Eric H. Cline, *From Eden to Exile: Unraveling Mysteries of the Bible* (Washington, DC: National Geographic Books, 2007), 17–29.

Kate Ravilious, "Noah's Ark Discovered in Iran?," *National Geographic News*, http://news.nationalgeographic.com/news/2006/07/060705-noahs-ark.html (posted July 5, 2006).

James K. Hoffmeier, "What is the Biblical Date for the Exodus? A Response to Bryant Wood," *Journal of the Evangelical Theological Society* 50/2 (2007): 225–47.

J. Maxwell Miller and John H. Hayes, *A History of Ancient Israel and Judah*, 2nd ed. (Louisville, KY: Westminster John Knox Press, 2006) 113–17.

William G. Dever, *Who Were the Early Israelites and Where Did They Come From?* (Grand Rapids, MI: Wm. B. Eerdmans Publishing Company, 2003), 194–200.

Israel Finkelstein and Neil A. Silberman, *The Bible Unearthed: Archaeology's New Vision of Ancient Israel and the Origin of Its Sacred Texts* (New York: Simon and Schuster, 2001) 99–122, 329–39.

Amnon Ben-Tor, "Excavating Hazor, Part I: Solomon's City Rises from the Ashes," *Biblical Archaeology Review* 25/2 (1999): 26–37, 60.

Amnon Ben-Tor, "The Fall of Canaanite Hazor—The 'Who' and 'When' Questions," in *Mediterranean Peoples in Transition: Thirteenth to Early Tenth Centuries BCE*, ed. Sy Gitin, Amihai Mazar, and Ephraim Stern (Jerusalem: Israel Exploration Society, 1998), 456–68.

Amnon Ben-Tor and Maria Teresa Rubiato, "Excavating Hazor, Part Two: Did the Israelites Destroy the Canaanite City?," *Biblical Archaeology Review* 25/3 (1999): 22–39.

Brian Hesse and Paula Wapnish, "Can Pig Remains be Used for Ethnic Diagnosis in the Ancient Near East?" in *The Archaeology of Israel: Constructing the Past, Interpreting the Present*, ed. Neil A. Silberman and David Small (Sheffield, UK: Sheffield Academic Press, 1997), 238–70.

Chapter 8

J. Maxwell Miller and John H. Hayes, *A History of Ancient Israel and Judah*, 2nd ed. (Louisville, KY: Westminster John Knox Press, 2006), 292, 294 (Text 3), 298, 307 (Text 5).

David Ussishkin, "Defensive Judean Counter-Ramp Found at Lachish in 1983 Season." *Biblical Archaeology Review* 10/2 (1984): 66–73.

———, *The Renewed Archaeological Excavations at Lachish (1973–1994)*, vol. 1–5 (Tel Aviv, Israel: Institute of Archaeology, Tel Aviv University, 2005), passim.

Erika Bleibtreu, "Five Ways to Conquer a City." *Biblical Archaeology Review* 16/3 (1990): 37–44.

———, "Grisly Assyrian Record of Torture and Death." *Biblical Archaeology Review* 17/1 (1991): 52–61, 75.

J. Maxwell Miller and John H. Hayes, *A History of Ancient Israel and Judah*, 2nd ed. (Louisville, KY: Westminster John Knox Press, 2006), 418–19 (Text 12), 443–44 (Text 15).

Oded Lipschits, "Demographic Changes in Judah between the Seventh and the Fifth Centuries B.C.E.," in *Judah and the Judeans in the Neo-Babylonian Period*, ed. Oded Lipschits and Joseph Blenkinsopp (Winona Lake, IN: Eisenbrauns, 2003), 364.

Chapter 9

Gabriel Barkay, Marilyn J. Lundberg, Andrew G. Vaughn, Bruce Zuckerman, and Kenneth Zuckerman, "The Challenges of Ketef Hinnom: Using Advanced Technologies to Reclaim the Earliest Biblical Texts and Their Context," *Near Eastern Archaeology* 66/4 (2003): 170.

Gabriel Barkay, Marilyn J. Lundberg, Andrew G. Vaughn, Bruce Zuckerman, and Kenneth Zuckerman, "The Amulets from Ketef Hinnom: A New Edition and Evaluation," *Bulletin of the American Schools of Oriental Research* 334 (2004): 61, 68.

Hershel Shanks, ed., *Understanding the Dead Sea Scrolls* (New York: Vintage Press, 1992), passim.

Jodi Magness, *The Archaeology of Qumran and the Dead Sea Scrolls*. (Grand Rapids, MI: William B. Eerdmans, 2002), passim.

Richard Bernstein, "Looking for Jesus and Jews in the Dead Sea Scrolls," *New York Times*, April 1, 1998.

Chapter 10

Robert J. Bull, "Caesarea Maritima: The Search for Herod's City," *Biblical Archaeology Review* 8/3 (1982): 24–40.

Amiram Barkat, "Researcher: We Have Found Herod's Tomb," *Ha'aretz*, May 8, 2007.

Press Release from the Hebrew University of Jerusalem, "Tomb of King Herod Discovered at Herodium by Hebrew University Archaeologist," May 8, 2007.

Josephus, *The Jewish War* 1.23.9, in *The New Complete Works of Josephus*, trans. William Whiston (Grand Rapids, MI: Kregel Publications, 1999), 670–73.

Jodi Magness, "Has the Tomb of Jesus Been Discovered?" Biblical Archaeology Society website, www.sbl-site.org/publications/article.aspx?articleId=640 (posted March 5, 2007).

Alan Cooperman, "'Lost Tomb of Jesus' Claim Called a Stunt," *Washington Post*, February 28, 2007, A3.

Laurie Goodstein, "Crypt Held Bodies of Jesus and Family, Film Says," *New York Times*, February 27, 2007.

Mark Chancey and Eric M. Meyers, "Spotlight on Sepphoris: How Jewish Was Sepphoris in Jesus' Time?" *Biblical Archaeology Review* 26/4 (2000): 18–33.

John C. H. Laughlin, "Capernaum: From Jesus' Time and After," *Biblical Archaeology Review* 19/5 (1993): 54–61.

Chapter 11

Shelley Wachsmann, "The Galilee Boat: 2,000-Year-Old Hull Recovered Intact," *Biblical Archaeology Review* 14/5 (1988): 19–33; see also Shelley Wachsmann, *The Sea of Galilee Boat: A 2000 Year Old Discovery From the Sea of Legends* (Cambridge, MA: Perseus Publishing, 1995).

Roni Reich, "Caiaphas Name Inscribed on Bone Boxes," *Biblical Archaeology Review* 18/5 (1992): 40–44, 76.

"Scholars Say John the Baptist Used This Cave For Immersions," *New York Times*, August 17, 2004.

Joe Zias, "The Cave of John the Baptist: John or Lazarus, the Patron Saint of Leprosy" (paper presented at the annual meetings of the American Schools of Oriental Research, Boston, MA, November 19–22, 2008).

Vassilios Tzaferis, "Inscribed 'To God Jesus Christ'; Early Christian Prayer Hall Found in Megiddo Prison," *Biblical Archaeology Review* 33/2 (2007): 42–43, 46.

Chapter 12

André Lemaire, "Une inscription paléo-hébraïque sur grenade en ivoire," *Revue Biblique* 88 (1981): 236–39; see also André Lemaire, "Probable Head of Priestly Scepter from Solomon's Temple Surfaces in Jerusalem; Inscription Containing Name of God Incised on Ivory Pomegranate," *Biblical Archaeology Review* 10/1 (1984): 24–29.

Yuval Goren, Shmuel Ahituv, Avner Ayalon, Miryam Bar-Matthews, Uzi Dahari, Michal Dayagi-Mendels, Aharon Demsky, and Nadav Levin, "A Re-examination of the Inscribed Pomegranate from the Israel Museum," *Israel Exploration Journal* 55/1 (2005): 3–20.

André Lemaire, "Burial Box of James the Brother of Jesus; Earliest Archaeological Evidence of Jesus Found in Jerusalem," *Biblical Archaeology Review* 28/6 (2002): 24–33.

Oded Golan, "Lecture at Cornerstone University in Grand Rapids, MI, April 2004," Biblical Archaeology Society website, http://web.archive.org/web/20060515120152/http://www.biblicalarchaeology.org/bswbOOossuary_Golan_Cornerstone.pdf.

Uzi Dahari, "Final Report of the Committees," Bible and Interpretation website, www.bibleinterp.com/articles/Final_committees_reports.htm.

Nadav Shragai, "The Art of Authentic Forgery," *Ha'aretz*, April 14, 2008; available online at www.haaretz.com/print-edition/features/the-art-of-authentic-forgery-1.243934.

Neil A. Silberman and Yuval Goren, "Faking Biblical History," *Archaeology* 56/5 (2003): 24.

David Noel Freedman, Shawna Dolansky Overton, and David Miano, "Jehoash Inscription," *Biblical Archaeology Review* (2004): 30/2: 50.

Hershel Shanks, "Assessing the Jehoash Inscription," *Biblical Archaeology Review* 29/3 (2003): 26–30.

Hershel Shanks, "Is It or Isn't It? King Jehoash Inscription Captivates Archaeological World," *Biblical Archaeology Review* 29/2 (2003): 22–23.

Shimon Ilani, Amnon Rosenfeld, and Michael Dvorachek, "Archaeometry of a Stone Tablet with Hebrew Inscription Referring to Repair of the House," *GSI Current Research* 13 (2003): 116.

Amnon Rosenfeld, Shimon Ilani, Joel Kronfeld, and Howard R. Feldman, "Archaeometric Analysis of the 'Jehoash Inscription' Stone Describing the Renovation of the First Temple of Jerusalem" (handout accompanying poster for paper no. 123–14 presented at the annual meetings of the Geological Society of America Annual Meeting, Salt Lake City, UT, October 16–19, 2005), abstract available online at http://gsa.confex.com/gsa/2005AM/finalprogram/abstract_90181.htm.

Shimon Ilani, Amnon Rosenfeld, Howard R. Feldman, Wolfgang E. Krumbein, Joel Kronfeld, "Archaeometric analysis of the 'Jehoash Inscription' tablet," *Journal of Archaeological Science* 35 (2008): 2966–72.

Yuval Goren, Avner Ayalon, Miryam Bar-Matthews, and Bettina Schilman, "Authenticity Examination of the Jehoash Inscription," *Tel Aviv* 31/1 (2004): 3, 13–14.

Uzi Dahari, "Final Report of the Committees," Bible and Interpretation website, www.bibleinterp.com/articles/Final_committees_reports.htm.

Kristin Romey, "Geologists: Ossuary Patina Faked," *Archaeology* magazine website www.archaeology.org/online/news/patina.html (posted June 23, 2003).

Bob Simon, "The Stone Box and Jesus' Brother's Bones;" CBS News broadcast, March 23, 2008; available online at www.cbsnews.com/video/watch/?id=3960839n&tag=mncol;1st;3 and www.cbsnews.com/stories/2008/03/20/60minutes/main3954980.shtml?tag=mncol;1st;1.

Nadav Shragai, "The Art of Authentic Forgery," *Ha'aretz*, April 14, 2008; available online at www.haaretz.com/print-edition/features/the-art-of-authentic-forgery-1.243934.

Neil Asher Silberman and Yuval Goren, "Faking Biblical History," *Archaeology* 56/5 (2003): 26.

Editor, online feature, "Gold Dust and James Bond: Israel Antiquities Authority Declares James Ossuary and Jehoash Inscription Fake," *Archaeology* magazine website, www.archaeology.org/online/features/ossuary/index.html (posted June 18, 2003).

Epilogue

Allyn Fisher-Ilan, "Goliath's Name Found in Archaeological Dig," Reuters (posted November 13, 2005).

Ron E. Tappy, "The Tel Zayit Inscription: An Archaeological Benchmark in the History of Writing," The Zeitah Excavations website, www.zeitah.net/UpdateTelZayit.html.

Yosef Garfinkel, "Qeiyafa Ostracon Chronicle," Khirbet Qeiyafa website, http://qeiyafa.huji.ac.il/ostracon.asp.

Inga Kiderra, "King Solomon's (Copper) Mines?: *Deep Dig Finds Confluence of Science and the Bible*," UC San Diego News Center, http://ucsdnews.ucsd.edu/newsrel/soc/10-22KingSolomon.asp (posted October 27, 2008).

Etgar Lefkovits, "Archaeologists Find Link to First Temple," *Jerusalem Post*, October 21, 2007.

Nadav Shragai, "Archaeologists Find Link to 1st Temple in Controversial J'lem Dig," *Ha'aretz*, October 21, 2007.

Etgar Lefkovits, "Jerusalem Affairs: Hard evidence," *Jerusalem Post*, September 27, 2007.

Nadav Shragai, "Antiquities Authority: Archaeologists Unearth Quarry Used to Renovate Second Temple," *Ha'aretz*, September 23, 2007.

Etgar Lefkovits, "Archeologists Find 2nd Temple Quarry," *Jerusalem Post*, September 23, 2007.

Nadav Shragai, "Archeologists Discover Segment of Jerusalem Drain from Second Temple Period," *Ha'aretz*, September 9, 2007.

Amy Teibel, "Archeologists Find Tunnel Used by Jews to Escape Roman Conquest of Jerusalem 2,000 Years Ago," *San Diego Union-Tribune*, September 9, 2007.

Further Reading

Albright, William F. *The Archaeology of Palestine and the Bible.* Cambridge, MA: Harvard University Press, 1932.

——. *From the Stone Age to Christianity: Monotheism and the Historical Process.* Baltimore: Johns Hopkins University Press, 1940.

Bahat, Dan. *The Illustrated Atlas of Jerusalem.* Jerusalem: Carta, 1996.

Ben-Tor, Amnon, ed. *The Archaeology of Ancient Israel.* New Haven: Yale University Press, 1992.

Biran, Avraham. *Biblical Dan.* New York: Hebrew Union College, 1994.

Borowski, Oded. *Daily Life in Biblical Times.* Atlanta: Society of Biblical Literature, 2003.

Burleigh, Nina. *Unholy Business: A True Tale of Faith, Greed and Forgery in the Holy Land.* New York: HarperCollins, 2008.

Crossan, John Dominic, and Jonathan L. Reed, *Excavating Jesus: Beneath the Stones, Behind the Texts.* Rev. ed. San Francisco: HarperSanFrancisco, 2001.

Davies, Philip R., George J. Brooke, and Phillip R. Callaway. *The Complete World of the Dead Sea Scrolls.* London: Thames & Hudson, 2002.

Davis, Miriam C. *Dame Kathleen Kenyon: Digging Up the Holy Land.* London: UCL Institute of Archaeology Publications, 2008.

Dever, William G. *What Did the Biblical Writers Know and When Did They Know It?: What Archaeology Can Tell Us About the Reality of Ancient Israel.* Grand Rapids, MI: Wm. B. Eerdmans Publishing Company, 2002.

Drower, Margaret S. *Flinders Petrie: A Life in Archaeology.* Madison, WI: University of Wisconsin Press, 1995.

Finegan, Jack. *The Archaeology of the New Testament: The Life of Jesus and the Beginning of the Early Church.* Rev. ed. Princeton, NJ: Princeton University Press, 1992.

Finkelstein, Israel, and Neil A. Silberman. *David and Solomon: In Search of the Bible's Sacred Kings and the Roots of the Western Tradition.* New York: Free Press, 2006.

Hoerth, Alfred J. *Archaeology and the Old Testament.* Grand Rapids, MI: Baker Books, 1998.

Hoffmeier, James K. *Israel in Egypt: The Evidence for the Authenticity of the Exodus Tradition.* Oxford: Oxford University Press, 1997.

Hoffmeier, James K. *Ancient Israel in Sinai: The Evidence for the Authenticity of the Wilderness Tradition.* Oxford: Oxford University Press, 2005.

Kenyon, Kathleen M. *Archaeology in the Holy Land.* 4th ed.. New York: W.W. Norton & Co Inc, 1979.

King, Philip J., and Lawrence E. Stager. *Life in Biblical Israel.* Louisville, KY: Westminster John Knox Press, 2001.

Kitchen, Kenneth A. *On the Reliability of the Old Testament.* Grand Rapids, MI: William B. Eerdmans Publishing Company, 2003.

Laughlin, John C. H. *Archaeology and the Bible.* London: Routledge, 2000.

McRay, John. *Archaeology and the New Testament.* Grand Rapids, MI: Baker Book House, 1991.

Netzer, Ehud. *The Architecture of Herod, the Great Builder.* Tübingen: Mohr Siebeck, 2006.

Petrie, William M. F. *Seventy Years in Archaeology.* London: Kegan Paul, 1931.

Shanks, Hershel, and Ben Witherington III. *The Brother of Jesus: The Dramatic Story & Meaning of the First Archaeological Link to Jesus & His Family.* San Francisco: HarperSanFrancisco, 2003.

Vanderkam, James, and Peter Flint. *The Meaning of the Dead Sea Scrolls: Their Significance for Understanding the Bible, Judaism, Jesus, and Christianity.* San Francisco: HarperSanFrancisco, 2002.

Yadin, Yigael. *Hazor: The Rediscovery of a Great Citadel of the Bible.* New York: Random House, 1975.

Biblical Archaeology

Index

Index

World War I (WW I), 20, 29, 30, 35
World War II (WW II), 35, 36, 40
Wright, G. Ernest, 53

Y

Yadin, Yigael, 42, 43, 44, 45, 46, 48,
    49, 64, 78, 92
Yardeni, Ada, 119
Yasur-Landau, Assaf, 67, 68

Yigal Allon Museum, 107

Z

Zayit, Tel, 131
Zertal, Adam, 51, 55
Zias, Joe, 49, 104, 111
Ziusudra, 73
Zuckerman, Bruce, 90
Zuckerman, Kenneth, 90